Williamina

For Love of Williamina

RALPH ROCHESTER

AGRE

For Barbara

First published in 2001
by AGRE BOOKS
Groom's Cottage, Nettlecombe,
Bridport, Dorset, DT6 3SS

www.agrebooks.co.uk

Typeset by Agre Books, printed and bound by
R. Booth Ltd, Mabe, Cornwall

ISBN 0 9538000 3 2

A CIP catalogue record for this book is available
from the British Library

CONTENTS

NO NEED OF VERSES

Our love has been for me, my dear,
our love has been for you,
both sun and moon, nor did we need
to ask if it were true;
it warmed our days, it lit our nights,
it was our world entire;
we had no need of verses then,
to kindle our desire.

And shall we now chirp rhapsodies
from ev'ry cliff and crag,
or roar out turgid mating-calls
alike the rutting stag,
or tell in golden numbers how
true love is lost or found?
We have no need of verses now,
when love is safe and sound.

And when time plays the thief and steals
the half of all we have,
we'll hue and cry until we lie
together in one grave;
and suns and moons shall rise and fall,
and seas and mountains move.
What shall we need of verses there,
to teach us how we love?

Ralph Rochester

William and Williamina

Love is its own great loveliness alway,
And takes new lustre from the touch of time;
Its bough owns no December and no May,
But bears its blossom into Winter's clime.

Thomas Hood

IN the winter of 1809 Williamina Forbes came to the small town of Lympstone in Devon. At the age of thirty-two, the life of this brave Scotswoman was already ending. In her youth she had been a bright beauty who had enraptured her young tutor, James Mill. Williamina's beauty had also broken the heart of a young Edinburgh advocate, Walter Scott, who was by now the most popular literary figure in Britain.

The Hundred of East Devon, like other corners of the West of England, had long offered sanctuary to fashionable invalids. There was sumptuous accommodation to be found fit for the households of stricken but wealthy exiles. Towns and villages near the Channel coast and inland along sheltered estuaries offered the prospect of warmth and sunshine where health-giving sea breezes could be freely inhaled. Lympstone on the River Exe below Exeter was such a place.

Williamina would probably have wandered even further from home if Britain had not again been at war with the French. She might have travelled across the Continent to breathe the salutary mountain air of Switzerland, or else melted away under a Riviera sun, there to be entombed in a white sarcophagus at the top of some ancient Mediterranean town; but war had once again closed the French ports and the grateful coastal towns of East Devon welcomed a steady supply of genteel, pathetic invalids who came, spent money and wasted away in Sidmouth and Salterton, Exmouth and Dawlish and a dozen other seaside or estuarial places that strove to maintain a reputation for health and healing.

The 1801 Peace of Amiens had threatened to reduce the supply of convalescents, but peace lasted only sixteen months and property agents in the south-west never ceased to advertise their houses as being 'peculiarly adapted for invalids', while the local tradesmen, together with the doctors, apothecaries, embalmers, undertakers, stonemasons, parsons, sextons, and gravediggers had all continued to be profitably engaged in the melancholy business that was a product of the dwindling spirits of well-off invalids.

Today, there are mossy tombstones and neglected headstones to be found in every seaside churchyard in East Devon bearing silent witness to this influx from the colder parts of the kingdom. Church walls are hung with many a mournful, marble memorial to lady, gentleman or child who 'died in this place', whose virtues and perfections and piety were necessarily unequalled, and who, after a long and cruel illness patiently borne - always patiently borne! - departed this life in the sure hope of finding peace at last and of attaining eternal life.

In the opening months of the year 1809, when Williamina was still in Edinburgh and unaware of her illness, she must have seemed to her acquaintance to be a favourite of fortune. Her full title was Williamina Belsches Wishart Stuart, Lady Forbes. She was rich, well-born, virtuous and still handsome and she was happily married to one of Edinburgh's most respected citizens, Sir William Forbes of Pitsligo. William and Williamina were known to be a devoted couple and they had five fine children. The eldest, Jane, was twelve years old and then came William, Eliza, Jack and Charles. It was already a large and happy family and that year Williamina discovered she was expecting another child.

The family home was Colinton House, which in those days was four miles outside the city. This great house was situated in its own park, separated and hidden from the surrounding roads by tall trees. Its pleasant gardens sloped down to the Water of Leith. Here, within their domestic circle, the Forbes lived a quiet, secluded, countrified life. In term-time, young William, the son and heir, was already being educated away from home at Peebles.

At Colinton there was a beloved governess, a Miss Ballingall, a minister's daughter from Banffshire, who was as much a friend of the family as she was a servant, and who cared for the education of the other four children.

The family's town house in Edinburgh was at 86 George Street, just around the corner from Walter Scott's house in Castle Street. The Forbes much preferred to spend their days at Colinton but early that year Williamina was declared 'delicate' by her physician and it was thought wise that Sir William should bring her into town for her confinement. Here on the 20 April a son was born, James David Forbes, who was at once introduced to the family as Jem.

Jem was safely delivered and was a strong, healthy baby, but shortly after his birth Williamina experienced night-sweats; she then developed a persistent dry cough and soon she noticed that she was losing weight. At some stage she developed a 'sad shake'. She had all too clearly contracted consumption, what today would be called tuberculosis of the lung, and she had to expect to 'submit to a decline'.

Tuberculosis of the lung, although it is a disease born of dirt and squalor, was never a respecter of persons. The tubercle bacilli are very tough and can lie dormant in dirt and dust for a long time until they resurrect themselves and seek out a new happy home in the human lungs. The unwitting victim breathes them in with the air. It was, no doubt, from some clarty corner of Edinburgh, a city famous throughout the realm for its total want of all faecal propriety, that a phalanx of virulent bacilli had sallied out and had been breathed in by Williamina. From that unhappy moment she entered on the last scene of her life.

During the advance of the cold winter of 1809 her physicians insisted that she should travel south to the warmth of Devonshire for the sake of her health. The best that she could do, they advised, was to quit the cold of Edinburgh for a warmer place and spend as much time as possible out-of-doors in the fresh air. This course of action had the advantage that the patient could hope for a recovery and an easement of her present pain while at the same time her other children, who were left behind in Scotland, were free from the risk of contagion.

Williamina had faith in the advice of her family and her physicians and did not doubt that she was doing the right and necessary thing. It was painful for her to abandon her home and to part from her children. She described her wandering as a sacrifice for which she hoped to be amply repaid by the blessing of health restored. It was her duty, and she was a great believer in duty, to try to recover from her disease, not for her own sake but for the sake of her young children. Her dearest wish was that she should soon return to Edinburgh to care for her growing family but for the time being she was prepared to sacrifice all of earthly enjoyment and to trust in the omnipresence of God.

Sir William, her husband, was the seventh baronet of an ancient line that had flourished in Scotland since the thirteenth century. The Forbes of Pitsligo were proud of their title, so proud of it that Sir William's father, another Sir William who had died in 1805, was known to have refused the offer of an Irish peerage in order to carry on being Forbes of Pitsligo in the eyes of the world. The present Sir William was a healthy, handsome, public-spirited man of thirty-five. In Edinburgh society he was respected as a sportsman, a traveller and a fine horseman. He was also the head of a famous banking-house and his fortune was assured. He had a quiet, reserved nature and an aversion to ostentation and display that made Walter Scott, who served with him as an officer of the Edinburgh Yeomanry, write that 'not Mimosa's tender tree / Shrinks sooner from the touch than he'. But his shyness only added to his charm and it was accepted that Sir William had a pleasing manner, was honest, generous and good company.

Sir William looked about for suitable accommodation for himself and his sick wife. At Lympstone he found and took a modern dwelling-house that offered every requisite for a gentleman's family. It had a coach-house, stables, cellars and a walled garden with an adjoining orchard stocked with the choicest fruit-trees and it had the advantage that it was close to Lympstone's health-giving shingle beach. Moreover it was within three minutes walk of the church. It stood above the Exe on a rise called Parsonage Hill among some of the finest houses in the village. With the house went a field, convenient for grazing horses. The rector of Lympstone, the Rev John Prestwood Gidoin, (pronounced 'Jedwin') lived nearby in Parsonage House, and another much-respected gentleman, Mr Wakelyn Welch and his wife Elizabeth, lived down the road. As part of the bargain went a large box-pew or seat in the church and, all in all, the house at Lympstone seemed fully able to meet the Forbes's requirements.

As the year drew to a close, Sir William undertook to take his sick wife down into Devonshire and, because nothing on this earth was going to part Williamina from her new baby, they took Jem with them, together with Lizzie Jervis who was the child's own nurse, one of the old Scotch type, stately and reserved, strict and conscientious, one who never went out to walk without her small well-worn bible in her pocket. There was also Jane, Williamina's favourite maid, and Mrs Elizabeth Ramage, a widow from Newhaven, who served as friend and companion to Williamina. Already waiting at Lympstone with clean linen and fires laid, was a Lympstonian, Mrs Georgiana Reynolds, who had been recommended to them as a housekeeper. She was the wife of William Reynolds, a gentleman of the parish who shared the rector's passion for shooting.

Sir William and Lady Forbes and their child, Jem, plus Lizzie and Jane, and Elizabeth Ramage travelled from Edinburgh, first staying in London and then, towards the end of November 1809, making the long journey by carriage, Sir William riding post, to follow the sun westwards to the relative warmth of Devon. The party's departure from London in their own carriage was delayed by Williamina having caught a disagreeable cold during a severe frost. At last it was considered that she was well enough to travel and on Friday 17 November they took to the road. Their plan was to travel in easy stages of never more than forty miles in a day. This meant that they did not finally arrive in Exeter until the 23rd. The rattling mail-coaches, by contrast, could be expected to deliver their passengers to Exeter, barring broken axle-trees, the loss of wheels and other accidents, within twenty-four hours.

The party travelled out of London in bitter winter weather and rumbled and rolled slowly over Bagshot Heath, a dreary moor extending for many miles without a mark of habitation and a waste not yet free of highwaymen. The turnpikes were still badly drained, poorly maintained and not yet built in accordance with Mr McAdam's system. The travellers made overnight stops at roadside inns, which Williamina found altogether unsatisfactory; the cold was intense and the inns were mere summer sheds. They spent the first night at Hartford Bridge where, a very few minutes after their arrival, it began to snow. They next stopped at Andover, where they were dismayed to find that the inn had no outer door, then they crossed 'that delectable desart y'cleped Salisbury

Plain' which Williamina described as 'something like what you may suppose a stormy sea suddenly arrested into solidity'. She later wrote to Jane, her eldest child: 'Frequently the horizon forms the only boundary of this cheerless scene, peopled by sheep, with here and there a few houses and a little cultivation.'

In freezing cold they came to Blandford, which Williamina found a wretched, cold, uncomfortable place and where she declared herself to be 'knocked up'. She was all over shooting pains and whenever she tried to breathe she felt as though she had been pierced from the heart-bone directly through the back. As soon as they arrived at the inn, she took to her unsatisfactory bed and only after eighteen hours 'stewing' did she feel able to journey on to Dorchester, in hopes of a better bed and of being nearer medical attention at Weymouth. In the event, she found Dorchester not much better than Blandford, but the next day, feeling somewhat recovered, the sad little party pushed on to reach Sidmouth, 'a most delightful spot', where 'beauty, cleanliness and comfort seemed united'. By now it was Wednesday. From Sidmouth they travelled the Roman road to Exeter and there William and Williamina spent two days collecting necessaries. They arrived in Lympstone on Friday, a full week after having left London.

On 3 December, nine days after her arrival, Williamina wrote from her new retirement to her father, Sir John Stuart. She declared that she found her 'little residence' in Lympstone 'very charming'. She found the rooms small but comfortable. The drawing room had 'little low windows looking to the south' and there was a sweet strawberry tree that enchanted her. Her bedroom entered from the drawing room and there was only just room enough to walk around the double bed and next to hers was a bedroom for the baby Jem where also slept Lizzie and Jane on tent-beds. The kitchen was next to the dining-room and had an earthen floor, quite hard and dry as if it had been baked.

Williamina was also pleased with the climate. The temperature was measured every day at eight in the morning and apart from the first morning when the thermometer stood at 25, 'which between cold and astonishment petrified the natives', the weather soon became so warm that she began to hope for an eventual recovery. She was enjoying the contrast between North and South Britain and it seemed to her that the neighbourhood must be a paradise in summer for 'even at this season it is very beautiful. The trees are not leafless neither are the leaves brown but retain a degree of greenness that throws over the general view that shade of verdure which precedes the bursting of the buds in spring and entirely takes off the appearance of December.'

She had already walked on the shingle-beach and looked across the calm December tides of the wide Exe to the deer-park and lawns and towers and turrets of Powderham Castle, home of the Earls of Devon, and had found it so wonderful a house that she declared it to be enough 'temptation to break the Tenth Commandment'. Best of all, the sharp pain from heart-bone to back which had cut her breath and which had particularly annoyed her during her journey, had first abated and then disappeared and, what was more, she felt that she was losing the sad shake that had greatly troubled her and which had 'reduced her more than she had ever yet been.' For the first time in many months she felt comfortably free of pain and was only too ready to attribute this to the move from Scotland to Devonshire. After her first week in Lympstone, her hopes of regaining her health and of returning to her children and her Scottish home had already been raised mightily.

TRAVELLING HOPEFULLY

We should roll westward when we look for hope,
crossing by warmer ways to where the seed
bursts forth, to where green hedgerows lead
to love and life, all on a sunnier slope

where seabirds soothe us with their grace and speed
and curlew calm us with their haunting call,
and we can stroll beside the rise and fall
of western rivers, while the red suns bleed

and there speak in fond hope, or not at all,
and promise rosier cheeks and brighter eyes,
and take our colour from the blushing skies
and praise the shadows that have grown so tall.

Yet even here, in hope, let us be wise
enough to keep in mind what fools forget:
for each of us, one sun shall never set,
or else a sun shall set, shall never rise.

Ralph Rochester

Lympstone in 1810

Let's all sing the Lymp-song
L-Y-M-P-STONE!
You can't go wrong with the Lymp-song
L-Y-M-P-STONE!
There's the old church clock and the Darling Rock
and the smell of the Exe ozone,
So, let's all sing the Lymp-song
L-Y-M-P-STONE!!

From the Lympstone Players' Pantomime c.1974
Words by James Moss

LYMPSTONE has been my home for nearly thirty-five years and seems to me to have always been a confident, self-possessed, good-humoured parish.

Imagine, if you will, a little old Georgian gentleman, neither rich nor poor, attending an assembly of the kind one finds in Jane Austen's novels. This gentleman has found a warm, pleasant spot near the fire and he means to stay there. In one hand he holds a glass of Madeira negus and, with elegant nonchalance, he has stuck the thumb of his other hand into his waistcoat pocket. He intends to have little to do with the world around him other than to observe with a bright eye the follies and fashions of the young and ambitious. He stands secure and steady with his legs well apart. He is not to be ruffled or shaken. If a neighbour speaks to him, he will respond with generous warmth but he hopes to escape without too much chat. Nevertheless, before the evening is over you can depend upon it he will have talked to every guest and he will have said a few kind words and he will be informed of all his neighbours' affairs. The punch bowl is at hand and nothing on earth will persuade him to join the dance or to seek out company, but he is as happy and contented as any in the room. To my mind this old gentleman is the Spirit of Lympstone.

Much has changed in the parish and the twenty-first century promises more changes which often threaten to be crass and potentially disastrous to the Spirit of Lympstone. But some things do go on for ever; the health-giving tidal banks across which blow south-westerly winds, the clear western skies that present the same glorious estuary sunsets which Francis Danby painted when he lived in Exmouth between 1841 and his death in 1861, the distant and ever changing views of Haldon Hills, the ebb and flow of the tide, the bubbling of the curlews and the calling of seabirds, the high, red sandstone cliffs fronting the estuary, the lush green of the Devon farmland and the babbling flow of the Wotton brook; these at least remain so little changed that the ghosts of Lympstone's dead parishioners could hardly mistake this corner of England for any other, were they to wander back from the far side of the grave.

In 1810 the parish began with Lympstone Lake,

which was a deep channel of the estuary where sizeable ships could approach and lie at anchor and send a boat ashore. Then there was the Cove, which provided a natural shelter for boats, big and small, and which sheltered a small quay where little ships could be laden and unladen. The Cove was surrounded by a scoop of red cliffs and a great gobbet of these, large enough to graze a few sheep, had been chipped away by wind and weather to form a small, rocky, grass-topped island. This was the Darling Rock where in 1792 Thomas Paine's *Rights of Man* was publicly burned. The loyal parishioners of Lympstone watched the ashes float away on the ebb-tide in the direction of Revolutionary France.

The sandstone cliffs of Lympstone were wonderfully craggy and weathered and crowned with wind-swept trees and scrub. Within and around the Cove were sheds and lockers where gear was stored and poles set out with lines where fishermen could dry and mend their nets. The shingle was littered with old chains and broken anchors and stinking fish-heads and dead, green crabs, and unwanted scad picked out of the nets, and a fair selection of domestic rubbish thrown from doors and windows.

On the foreshore near the Quay were two working limekilns that stank of burning lime, and several slipways, and the sheds of small shipyards. Here was a huddle of cottages of mariners and fisherfolk and a poor-house. The houses here were for the most part overcrowded hovels, low, mean, damp and poorly-thatched. To seaward were wooden jetties sporting an untidy jumble of lobster pots and other fishing gear. At the top of one narrow alley was a parish pump to which the fishermen's wives and daughters carried their pails for fresh water. Here and there and beside the brook that flowed beneath a bridge into the estuary, were one or two houses of some pretension, with brick or stone walls and perhaps a carriageway. There were two alehouses, the White Swan and the New Inn.

Flooding was a regular occurrence in this part of the village and could be expected whenever there was a gale from the west and the tides were high and there came a simultaneous downpour of rain to swell the brook. These floods invaded the cottages by day or night and covered the cobbled streets for many hours between tides while miserable people splashed through the shallows and happy ducks swam between the houses.

The village road, the Strand, ran parallel to the river. Other narrow cobbled lanes cut down to the water's edge. The Strand was a busy street with many shops and businesses and it rose eastwards towards terraces of small, newish, red-brick houses. Fronting these tidy cottages were small, fenced front-gardens which in summer were full of jasmine, roses, honeysuckle and red-blossomed japonica. There was a sharp turning high up on the left, up a steep, narrow, twisting lane, that curved past the Rector's grand house on Parsonage Hill. This was the road towards Exeter. Here on the hill was also the house taken by William and Williamina. Some of the neighbouring residences, like the parsonage itself, were ancient homes showing the influence of many styles and fashions, but Sir William's house was not one of these. It was a sensible, modern, square, red-brick building with a façade boasting three rows of windows, fourteen in all, and with a white-pillared porch at the front door. The road in front of Williamina's windows had once run on pleasantly beside the banks of the Exe between the great house, Nutwell Court, and the shore. But now there was a new road and a high wall built that skirted Lord Heathfield's great estate of Nutwell. This arrangement spared the household at Nutwell from the curious gaze of rude Lympstonians and at the sharp corner where the road had been blocked and turned there was now a lodge and gate standing sentry.

Back along the Strand and further up the village street there were more large houses, old and new, with fine gardens, orchards and grazing, rich with trees and hedgerows, Finally, beyond the lower village, was the ancient Church of the Nativity of the Blessed Virgin Mary.

The church appeared to Williamina much as we see it illustrated overleaf. In 1814, William Spreat, bookseller of Exeter, married Jane Warren, a yeoman farmer's daughter of Lympstone. Young William Spreat whisked Jane Warren away to the big city of

Lympstone Church by W. Spreat (1840)

Exeter, to be sweet and neat for Mr Spreat in and out
of the shop, (Spreat's was next to Spratt's the Tinman,
in the High Street.) There Jane Spreat reflected her
husband's glory as a freeman and later as a steward of
that city and, later yet, (great was the honour), as
librarian to the Devon and Exeter Botanical and
Horticultural Society. It was Jane's eldest son, William
Spreat junior, who made this fine drawing of the
church in 1840 when he was a very young man right
at the start of his career.

Happily, young William Spreat managed to sketch
Lympstone church before the great rebuilding of 1864.
He was a considerable artist and an inveterate
lithographer of churches who in his time managed to

record half the churches of Devon, but he had a special love for this particular church where his grandfather worshipped and where his parents had been married.

In 1810, the church in Lympstone, though neat and decent and superior to most churches in the vicinity, compared unfavourably with the spacious and elegant parish churches of Edinburgh. For William and Williamina however it held a certain rustic charm. Their short walk to church beneath fine trees, across lush meadows was delightful. The path they trod is still there but today it runs between a housing estate and a playing field. Williamina came down to the church by a path that crossed a churchyard shaded by pensive yews. She passed beneath the ancient red tower, which was as remarkably high as the nave was remarkably low, and she entered into a gloom that was intriguingly antique; this despite the fact that the church had within the last fifty years been awkwardly filled with box-pews and galleries and a triple-decker pulpit after the Georgian fashion. These pews and galleries had grown haphazardly so that they now obscured the ancient wall paintings and cut out much of the light, to such a degree that during the winter months the Rector could scarcely see to perform the service and Mr Richard Fley, the clerk, could not see unless he opened the door of his desk. It was intended to let in a skylight in the northern roof of the south aisle in order to convey more light to the pulpit, but this did not happen during Williamina's short stay.

On the wall of the north aisle there was, half-visible, a medieval mural of St Christopher carrying the Christ-child across the river, a depiction often to be found in churches near fords or navigable waters. Above the handsome altarpiece there was an ancient rood-loft, reached by narrow steps. What little could still be seen of the fabric of the old church was painted in green, vermilion and blue, and in the north aisle there were some old painted panes including a St George with the inscription – 'the holy knight, / Who slew the dragon by his might.' Within the church were tombs to Drakes and Fords and Lees and Egertons.

During divine service, the church was always full, with benches set out for the villagers in every free space. Those poor souls who sat up in the galleries had long complained that they could not breathe for want of air, but nothing had been done about it. Down below, the gentle families, and the would-be genteel, were tucked away like so many pigeons inside the walls of their boxes. Music was piped from flutes and scraped from fiddles and from the cracked bass-viol played by Henry Crabb, shoemaker, and from the tall, fifteenth-century tower a ring of five musical bells called the faithful to prayer and pealed out for weddings and holidays. When told of a death, the sexton tolled the death-bell. A muffled knell would be rung for Williamina.

A quarter mile east of the church, a lane, in part badly overhung with untrimmed trees, crossed the busy turnpike from Exeter to Exmouth. Around this crossroads was the cluster of small thatched houses which constituted Upper Lympstone. At this crossroads might be found farmers and husbandmen in their smocks and leggings, and farmers' wives and daughters bound for market with the produce of the farm, and sportsmen and gamblers and traders and all the horse and foot travellers who came along the turnpike. Here was the stage where the mail-coach halted daily to take up and set down passengers and parcels, packets and letters, and here were a busy roadhouse, smithy, saddlery and malthouse.

The country to the east beyond the road was of pleasant, rounded hills with fields and brakes and plantations and extensive game-preserves where pheasants clattered in the coverts and where poachers risked the man-traps set by gamekeepers. Here too were the high-hedged lanes that allowed glimpses of the essential glory of Devon: 'O England' wrote the child-poet Sarah Weymouth of Collaton. 'Thy fruitful gardens and thy cultured fields / Bespeak the hand of industry around: / While every hill a waving harvest yields, / And in thy valleys flocks and herds abound.'

Between these hills, a track wandered up beside the brook to the borders of the high commons where one or two isolated cottages were being built by pioneers and where land was still being enclosed, an acre at a time, to serve as fresh pasturage and tillage at the instance of a philanthropic landowner, Lord Rolle, who held that by withdrawing the cottager from his haunts in the village, time that would otherwise have been spent at the ale-house or in frivolous conversation with neighbours would be employed to the immediate benefit of himself and his family. Here too, in the corner where the parish met the common, there were good-sized, newly-won plots where the poor cottagers of Lympstone, if they were prepared to make the long walk, could grow potatoes and keep pigs.

The remaining high wastes offered fine views of river and sea. Here there was nothing but bracken and scrub with some clumps of fir and deciduous trees. The able-bodied peasants, man, woman and child, climbed to these commons from the village below to seek fuel. They gathered fallen branches and picked wintry faggots from the thorn and then trudged the two miles home again, heavy-burdened. Sportsmen hunted here with dog and gun and there were ancient trackways where it was wiser not to travel alone or after dark. Rogues and vagabonds, bands of ragged gypsies and men and women without parishes passed this way.

This was the parish of Lympstone in 1810 from top to toe. To William, who was so shy, and Williamina, who was so unwell, everything seemed very different from home. They were dwelling among strangers and were desperately seeking comfort in their new home. Lympstone was certainly curious and outlandish to their eyes, but the Forbes had travelled in England before. In 1808 Charles Vancouver wrote that he considered the inhabitants of this part of Devon to demonstrate an 'openness of heart' and a 'mildness of character' which was 'not to be excelled in any part of England'. Those natives with whom the Forbes needed to deal could, with some small difficulty, be understood.

Williamina was by nature inclined to be pleased and as the weather became warmer she made daily excursions on foot and breathed in the Exe ozone and hoped to improve. She allowed herself to be driven out and about in her carriage through Lympstone's narrow lanes and beyond the parish boundaries and she lived here as happily as her illness and her separation from her children permitted.

STEPPING HOME BY MOONLIGHT

Stepping home by moonlight
down along the brook,
there us meets a pheasant
asking to be took;
asking to be took, boys,
and who would say 'en nay?
Pop 'en in the tetty-sack,
to help us on our way!

Stepping home by moonlight,
by the farmer's gate,
there us meets some hens' aigs
begging to be ate;
begging to be ate, boys,
and who would say 'em nay?
Put 'em in the tea-kiddle,
to help us on our way!

Stepping home by moonlight,
up the parson's wall,
there us meets some peaches
praying for a fall;
praying for a fall, boys,
and who would say 'em nay?
Wrap them in a hankerchee,
to help us on our way!

Stepping home by moonlight,
all along the tide,
there us meets a sammon
looking for a ride;
looking for a ride, boys ,
and who would say 'en nay?
Stow 'en in the bass-boat,
to help us on our way.

Ralph Rochester

James Mill and Williamina

My heart is sair, I dare not tell,
My heart is sair for somebody;
I could wake a winter night,
For the sake o'somebody!
Oh-hon! for somebody!
Oh hey! for somebody!
I could range the world around,
For the sake of somebody.

Robert Burns

IN November 1809, when William and Williamina passed through London on their way to Devonshire. James Mill, the philosopher, writer, editor, encyclopaedist, contributor to the *Edinburgh Review*, reformer and general master-mind, was thirty-five and had been living in a small house in Pentonville since 1805. He was, by now, well into writing his great work, the *History of India*, his marriage was unhappy, his family was growing and he had relatively recently met the great and wealthy Jeremy Bentham whose patronage he was beginning to enjoy.

James Mill and Williamina Forbes had been good friends since childhood, and marriage had not interrupted that friendship. Sir William Forbes had been useful to James in 1803 when James was trying to launch his publication, the *Literary Journal*, and James for his part had just reviewed William's father's book *The Life of Beattie,* for the *Edinburgh Review.* It is likely that the Forbes made a point of visiting James while they were in London. James was also a favourite with Williamina's parents.

Williamina's mother and father married in 1775 and she was born on 6 October the following year. All her life until her marriage, her family had suffered the name Belsches, though they bore it proudly. Then, in the year that Williamina married William Forbes, Sir John Belsches changed his name for the better and became known thereafter as Sir John Stuart. He was a devout Episcopalian and a high Tory, whom Scott's biographer Carola Oman describes as 'a cold and gloomy man, suffering from a sense of inferiority.' In the 1880s, James Mill's biographer Professor Bain went to the country around the Stuart's home at Fettercairn to inquire about Sir John and found that few people could give any account of him. He had not even been honoured with a newspaper paragraph at his death. The popular tradition made him out to be haughty and ill-tempered, but after hearing all that could be said in the locality, Professor Bain concluded that Sir John was a just-minded and generous man, though one who was somewhat imperious and who could not bear to be thwarted.

Certainly, although Sir John was a landowner and an advocate and, from 1802 to 1807, the Member of Parliament for Kincardineshire and after that a Baron of the Exchequer, he was also a deeply anxious man who was burdened with debt at the time when Williamina was growing up. He saw his only daughter as something of an investment for the future, an asset, a girl to be brought up to make a good match, and he took great care to make sure that she didn't kick over the traces. When William Forbes became Sir John's son-in law he rose to the occasion, generously managed all Sir John's financial problems, set all to rights quietly and without fuss, and did much good by stealth but had little enough thanks for it.

Lady Jane Stuart was said to be revered for every virtue, and she and some other pious women had started a fund for educating poor men for the ministry. This, apparently, was how the family at Fettercairn came to know the young James Mill, whose father, a country shoemaker, lived only five miles to the south of them in a dismal hamlet called Northwater Bridge. James was recommended to the Stuarts by the local church minister as being an exceptionally bright child and Sir John and Lady Jane, who had no son, came to take a close interest in him. He later made an admirable tutor for Williamina.

James Mill's home-life was impoverished. His mother's father had come down a little in the world after the Forty-Five Rebellion and his mother was known for her truly lady-like quality of disdaining good porridge. Her neighbours chiefly remembered her for saying: 'If you give me porridge, I'll die, but give me tea and I'll live.' She had determined that one day her eldest son would restore the family fortunes, but she seems to have been quite resigned that her other children, William and May, would live out their miserable lives at Northwater Bridge. James was to be a scholar and to this end his mother nurtured, petted and encouraged him, exempting him from all household duties. He was taught at the parish school and then at the Montrose Academy. He worked hard and excelled in all his studies and at some point he was scrubbed and marched, like Pip in *Great Expectations*, up to the great house, half castle, half stately-home, that was Fettercairn. This quasi-adoption probably took place very early on in his life. James Mill himself writes of his having 'grown up' with Williamina and of them having been 'children' together.

Williamina and her parents spent summers at Fettercairn and winters in Edinburgh. When he reached 18, Mill was encouraged by Sir John to study at Edinburgh, and thus to continue as Williamina's tutor. Sir John and Lady Jane had by now become strongly attached to him and he was always welcome in their homes and at their table.

In 1817 Mill wrote to the one friend in whom he confided, the reforming tailor Francis Place:

> As for Sir John Stuart, he is one of the Barons of the Exchequer in Scotland, and his estate and residence was near my father's. I was, at an early

age taken notice of by him and Lady Jane. When the time came for my going to college, it was my father's intention to send me to Aberdeen, as both nearer and less expensive than Edinburgh. Sir John, however and Lady Jane, insisted that he should let them take me to Edinburgh which was the more celebrated university; that they would look after me, and take care that the expense to my father should not be greater than at Aberdeen. I went to Edinburgh, and from that time lived as much in their house as in my father's, and there had many advantages, saw the best company, and had an educated man to direct my education, and who paid for several expensive branches of education, but which for him I must have gone without, and above all, had unlimited access in both town and country to well-chosen libraries. So you see I owe much to Sir John Stuart, who had a daughter, one only child, about the same age as myself, who besides being a beautiful woman, was in point of intellect and disposition one of the most perfect human beings I have known. We grew up together and studied together from children, and were about the best friends that either of us ever had.

Now there can be no doubt that young Williamina was a very fetching and desirable little poppet. She was a charming, plumpish lass with a mass of brown curly hair and a round, pretty, rather pert, intelligent face and a liveliness combined with seriousness that charmed her admirers. Her lashes were dark, her bright eyes were hazel-blue, her cheeks were full, her complexion was pale and she blushed easily. She had a good high forehead, half hidden by the nut-brown curls which were piled high on her head and tied up with a riband or snood, and she was often serious or pensive. She was well-dressed and she was very soon well-enough endowed with white swelling breasts, which fashion required to be raised up on wadding and whalebone as close to the chin as possible. She was highly intelligent, quick to learn, well-read and well-educated and accomplished in the arts. She was pious and virtuous and was even more dutiful than she was beautiful and her mild expression and downcast eye gave that impression of meekness and resignation to the will of others that was expected of the well-bred daughter of a good house. But, bless me! Williamina could be merry too and, when it was her duty so to do, she would sing and dance and laugh with the best of them and it was then that she was roguish and at her most charming and delightful.

This then was the girl with whom the young James Mill lived and worked closely for maybe as many as a dozen years. Even the ever-cautious Victorian logician and biographer Professor Bain suspected that Mill might have been smitten by Williamina. He wrote of the relationship that at a time when Williamina had reached 'an interesting age, she made a lasting impression on his mind. And that he spoke of her in later years with some warmth; putting it in the form of her great kindness to him.'

In later life James Mill was not a man famed for the warmth of his sentiments. His mind, says his biographer, was 'chiefly a compound of Intellect and Will. The Emotions were not wanting, but they were not the dominant interest.' Other commentators, notably Jeremy Bentham, but also members of his own family, have been less generous to him. The novelist Thomas Love Peacock made fun of his inability to like anything or anybody and many considered that in him, the milk of human kindness had long since gone off. Indeed, his expressions of feeling for Williamina are quite out of character and are also therefore probably something of an understatement. He also later had a reputation for being a humourless man who bullied his wife and children and who applied his own dour views on education to his own eldest son, thereby bringing him, in 1826, to have a nervous breakdown. This, however, did not perhaps do the boy any great harm for, of course, he was to become the yet greater philosopher and reformer, J. S. Mill.

It was at Sir John Stuart's request that Mill named this eldest son, born in 1806, John Stuart Mill and Sir John and Lady Jane continued to take an interest in the Mill family and, whenever they were in London, they made a point of visiting the Mills. Lady Jane wrote letters to Dear James, her only concern being that the old radical might be losing his faith in God, and as late as 1821 just before he died, Sir John Stuart sent a silver cup to John Stuart Mill, his 'godson', as Bain calls him, and also a present of £500 with the ostensible aim of sending John Mill to Cambridge. To this James Mill is reported to have said that his son was already so learned that there was nothing that Cambridge could teach him.

James Mill named his second child and eldest daughter, who was born in 1808, Williamina (or Wilhelmina) Forbes Mill, after the Baron's daughter with whom he seems to have been more than half in love. At home, Wilhelmina Mill's pet name was Willie (I do not believe that Williamina Forbes ever answered to this sweet diminutive! At times she was a Mina). Mill's sixth child, Jane, was named after Williamina's mother.

Mill had a brilliant mind. He was eloquent, impressive, earnest and energetic and his conversation was electrifying. It is fascinating to conjecture what power he had over young Williamina's thoughts and feelings, especially so if we imagine that he was all the time repressing a healthy lust for the gaucy lass. He certainly controlled her studies and must have done much to form her character. In the 1817 letter to Place quoted above, he claimed a remarkable secret sympathy with her, writing of being best friends. 'So much for the old friendship with Sir J Stuart, which it is very proper you should know, but which I do not wish to be talked about.'

When, in February 1802 at the age of twenty-nine,

Mill went off to London, he accompanied Williamina's father, the Member for Kincardineshire, who was obliged to attend the Parliament from 1802 till 1807. Without this stimulus, it seems unlikely that James would ever have made the move south. He seems to have found his own diggings in London fairly quickly, but it was Sir John who provided for his journey from Scotland, who supplied franking for his letters and who obtained admission to the gallery of the House of Commons, a privilege which he used freely.

A mischievous rumour was put about in London that Mill was Sir John's illegitimate son, but this was not believed by any who knew them in Scotland. If he had been so, and had, therefore, been Williamina's half-brother, their relationship would have been remarkably similar to that in Scott's *Redgauntlet* between the Lady Green Mantle and Darsie Latimer:

> 'Surely,' she replied; 'but were it not as easy for you to have said, to your own sister?'
> Darsie started in his saddle as if he had received a pistol shot.
> 'My sister!' he exclaimed.
> 'And did you not know it then?' said she.

Of such stuff romances are made, but it would have to be a strong plot to account for how the infant Mill came to be already living at Northwater Bridge four years before Sir John came to Fettercairn!

It must have been made clear to both Mill and

Williamina that all sexual desires had to be firmly subjugated. James was an attractive youth. He dressed carefully, had a fine figure, thought of himself as a gallant and bore himself like a gentleman; but at Fettercairn he was very conscious of being little more than a servant among servants and, however condescending Sir John and Lady Jane might be, he was no fool and he made sure that he did not risk his position there. His salvation lay in his ambition and in his natural coolth. In all his time as her friend and tutor he seems not to have put a foot or, more to the point, a hand, wrong. Williamina, for her part, knew what duty meant. More than anything else in the world, it meant not suffering any serious disagreeable consequences from the warmth of her temper. What also helped them both was their common belief, at this time, in a jealous God and in the fires of hell.

Williamina's other boyfriend during the seven years from 1790 to 1797 was young Walter Scott. Mill and Scott were much of an age, but if Mill had begun to glow in the world by the time Williamina came to Devonshire in 1810, Scott had risen like a meteor and was still rising. His incredible climb to fame and fortune was such that it requires a chapter to itself.

THE HARP

I was a wild and wayward boy,
My childhood scorn'd each childish toy;
Retired from all, reserved and coy,
To musing prone,
I woo'd my solitary joy,
My Harp alone.

My youth, with bold Ambition's mood,
Despised the humble stream and wood
Where my poor fathers's cottage stood,
to fame unknown;
What should my soaring views make good?
My Harp alone!

Love came with all his frantic fire,
And wild romance of vain desire:
The baron's daughter heard my lyre,
and praised the tone; -
What could presumptuous hope inspire?
My harp alone!

At manhood's touch the bubble burst,
And manhood's pride the vision curst,
And all that had my folly nursed
Love's sway to own;
Yet spared the spell that lull'd me first,
My Harp alone!

Woe came with war, and want with woe;
And it was mine to undergo
Each outrage of the rebel foe:
Can aught atone
My fields laid waste, my cot laid low?
My Harp alone!

Ambition's dreams I've seen depart,
Have rued of penury the smart,
have felt of love the venom'd dart
When hope was flown;
Yet rests one solace to my heart, -
My Harp alone!

Then over mountain, moor and hill,
My faithful harp, I'll bear thee still
And when this life of want and ill
Is well-nigh gone,
Thy strings mine elegy shall thrill,
My Harp alone!

from Rokeby *by Walter Scott*

The Venom'd Dart

Ah me! for ought that ever I could read,
Could ever hear by tale or history,
The course of true love never did run smooth!
A Midsummer Night's Dream

IN 1810 Walter Scott was thirty-eight, three years older than Sir William Forbes of Pitsligo and four years older than Williamina. He and William were old friends. Only one month after the Forbes's wedding, with the fear of a French invasion becoming every day more serious, they had both offered to serve with a freshly recruited body of volunteer cavalry to be known as the Edinburgh Light Horse. William was appointed as a cornet and Walter as the quartermaster. As fellow officers, they messed together whenever the Light Horse were in quarters and they were in the field together on manoeuvres. They experienced that comradeship that is the best part of any kind of soldiering.

It is difficult to overstate just how popular Scott had become by the year that Williamina Forbes was ill and exiled in Lympstone. Scott, who had grown up in Edinburgh, had not seemed a particularly promising youth. He had not excelled at the High School and he had enjoyed the reputation of being something of a wild and wayward boy who sometimes drank and brawled and roistered more than was good for him.

Scott was known by some of the lads as 'the Lamiter' because he had been lame since infancy and his remarkable will to win was in part a reaction to this infirmity. His family was respectable and had good connections. His parents were gentlefolk but were not wealthy and Walter was a younger son. Although he buckled down to trying to make a career for himself as a lawyer, his prospects did not seem all that glowing when, on Christmas Eve 1797, he married a pretty Frenchwoman, Charlotte (Charpentier) Carpenter, whom he had met only five months earlier.

By diligently exploiting his connections, Scott succeeded in being elected to the post of the Sheriff-Depute of Selkirkshire, an appointment that gave him a status he enjoyed and an income of £300 a year, an income he badly needed now that he was starting to raise a family.

He had started publishing verse when he was in his mid-twenties and his collections of ballads and occasional poems were reasonably popular and brought him some small fame, a little money and many literary friends. But then suddenly in 1805, to his own surprise and everybody else's, Scott caught the imagination of the entire reading public of the United Kingdom with the publication of his long poem, *The Lay of the Last Minstrel*. This strange tale of goblins, enchantments and border savagery is set in Branksome Hall, otherwise Branxholm Castle in Roxburghshire, an ancient seat of the Buccleuchs where remarkable events took place in the middle of the sixteenth century. For some reason the poem appealed immediately to all who read it and in a matter of weeks Scott found himself the most popular writer in Britain.

In no time at all his book had sold many thousands of copies. No-one had ever seen such sales for a poem, and it was praised by all who read it. Among those who extolled the work were those old political enemies William Pitt and George Fox, the leading Tory and the leading Liberal of the day, who barely had time to lay down the *Lay* before it was time for the undertakers to lay them down, side by side, in Westminster Abbey. More to the point, even the poets and writers and critics of the age were more or less unanimous in their praise of the work and the fortunate young bard was swamped with letters of congratulation. As Scott later neatly expressed it, 'the author had to perform a task difficult to human vanity, when called upon to make the necessary deductions from his own merits, in a calm attempt to account for his popularity.'

Nowadays it is difficult to imagine such glory for a writer. The written word in Georgian Britain did not compete, as it does today, with a dozen other forms of entertainment. Popular books were consumed with passion and their sequels awaited with lively anticipation, and, once published, popular works stayed popular for years rather than months. At that time the entire population of the United Kingdom of Great Britain and Ireland numbered only some eleven million and the reading public was only a tiny élitist fraction of this. A run of a few thousand copies could stir the literate nation. Copies of the *Lay* were passed from hand to hand and the poem excited great interest and comment. It was the custom at soirées for those who could not sing or play to recite a few stirring lines of poetry. Purple passages from the *Lay* were declaimed with dramatic gesture and in stirring tones in drawing-rooms up and down the land. Mr Scott's work gave so much pleasure that there was already talk in high places of making him a baronet for the sake of his art, but it was not until 1820 that he became Sir Walter Scott.

One of the charms of Scott's work is his portrayal of the longings and the disappointments of young lovers and the pangs and passions of those unlucky in love. His love-affairs are always maudlin and often there is a pure note of romantic anguish. One of the criticisms that Scott levelled against himself, and one of the reasons why he later turned to the writing of novels, was that in his romantic poems he never managed to achieve the emotional depths of, for example, Byron. This is true, but there is one sentiment that he portrays artlessly and in a few well-chosen words over and over again. This is the desolation felt by a thwarted or spurned lover.

His heroine in *The Lay of the Last Minstral* is Margaret of Branksome, a tall, blue-eyed blonde. She has a scheming witch of a mother, who is determined to part her from her lover, Henry Cranstoun, and Margaret knows well that 'her mother dread / Before Lord Cranstoun she should wed / Would see her on her dying bed.' From the anguish of these lovers Scott distils perhaps the most beautiful lines he ever wrote:

> True love's the gift which God has given
> To man alone beneath the heaven:
> It is not fantasy's hot fire,
> Whose wishes, soon as granted, fly;
> It liveth not in fierce desire
> With dead desire it doth not die;
> It is the secret sympathy,
> The silver link, the silken tie,
> Which heart to heart and mind to mind
> In body and in soul can bind.

This great romantic ideal of a true love between two people that is an indestructible bond, independent of and greater than all desires and all circumstances including death, is the credo that underlines and lends conviction to many of his simplest lines. Scott believed in the 'silver link and silken tie' because he knew all about it from his own experience.

Three years after *The Lay of the Last Minstrel*, Scott's poem *Marmion* was published to tremendous public acclaim. The poem took its place in history as the first modern best-selling publication and caused a sensation when Constable paid the huge sum of £1,000 unseen to publish it. *Marmion* was another strange tale from the sixteenth century with, among other wonders, a nun who disguises herself as a page-boy and has the great misfortune to be walled-up alive. There are many complex villainous plots and counter-plots which clearly gave the public precisely what it had been waiting for, and Scott became more popular than ever. The book sold 34,000 copies between 1808 and 1825 and Scott was lionised in London and in Edinburgh.

Once again the literary world was loud in his praise. Wordsworth, who had already met Scott and who subscribed himself as Scott's friend, 'for such I will call myself, though slow to use such a word of solemn meaning to anyone' had enjoyed a recitation of *Marmion* by Scott before publication. It is true that the young Lord Byron objected both to *The Lay of the Last Minstrel* and to *Marmion* and particularly to the fact that Scott was earning so much money from his writing. '*Lays of Minstrels* – may they be the last!' he fumed. Byron laughed at Scott's tales of terror that made dames to 'skip at every step, God knows how high / And frighten foolish babies, God knows why!' He went on to write:

These are the themes that claim our plaudits now;
These are the bards to whom the muse must bow;
  While Milton, Dryden, Pope, alike forgot
  Resign their hallow'd bays to Walter Scott.

Hurtful though Byron's insulting squibs might have been, his lone voice was hardly to be descried amid the rapturous applause that Scott received.

The heroine of *Marmion* is the Lady Clare, of whom we learn only that she is 'lovely, and gentle and distress'd'. But perhaps the best thing in *Marmion* is the 'song' *Lochinvar,* which once every schoolboy knew and which was recited in many a Georgian drawing-room. Here too the theme is of a disappointed suitor who because of his courage and daring and because of the secret sympathy that exists between him and the fair Ellen, his 'true love', is able to win back his own sweetheart against all the odds.

And now, at the beginning of the year 1810, with Williamina facing decline and death, Scott was putting the finishing touches to his new poem, *The Lady of the Lake*, a work that would again break all records for published verse and raise him to the very pinnacle of his fame and his fortune. The book would come out in the May and would be an elegant publication with a handsome portrait of Scott as frontispiece. Once again there was to be a heroine and a hero to woo her and, this time, two rivals to be discomforted. This time his heroine, another Ellen, is a raven-haired, dark-eyed beauty.

Ellen is the Lady of the Lake who, of course, is also forced to conceal her true love for a gallant:

'One only passion unreveal'd, / With maiden pride the maid conceal'd, / Yet not less purely felt the flame;-

/ O need I tell that passion's name?' There was to be
another romantic poem and another curly-headed
heroine. *Rokeby* is set during the English Civil War
and did not appear until 1812, two years after the death
of Williamina. The scene is Yorkshire immediately
after the battle of Marston Moor. This time the
heroine is called Matilda and is lovingly described
thus:

> Wreath'd in its dark-brown rings, her hair
> Half hid Matilda's forehead fair,
> Half hid and half reveal'd to hue
> Her full dark eye of hazel hue.
> The rose, with faint and feeble streak,
> So slightly tinged the maiden's cheek,
> That you had said her hue was pale;
> But if she faced the summer gale,
> Or spoke, or sung, or quicker moved,
> Or heard the praise of those she loved,
> Or when of interest was express'd
> Aught that waked feeling in her breast,
> The mantling blood in ready play
> Rivall'd the blush of rising day.
> There was a soft and pensive grace,
> A cast of thought upon her face,
> That suited well the forehead high,
> The eyelash dark, and downcast eye;
> The mild expression spoke a mind
> In duty firm, compos'd resign'd;
> 'Tis that which Roman art has given
> To mark their maiden Queen of Heaven.

In hours of sport, that mood gave way
To Fancy's light and frolic play;
And when the dance, or tale, or song,
In harmless mirth sped time along,
Full oft her doating sire would call
His Maud the merriest of them all.

Years later in 1818, Scott wrote to his pen-friend, Maria Edgeworth, the author of *Castle Rackrent* (on the same day he wrote much the same letter to the celebrated *Ladies of Llangollen*). 'This much of Matilda I recollect – (for that is not so easily forgotten)- that she was attempted for the existing person of a lady who is now no more, so that I am particularly flattered with your distinguishing it from the others, which are in general mere shadows.'

The lady he refers to here can only be Williamina Forbes. Scott had been in love with her from the first day he saw her, when she was fifteen, and he was obsessed with memories of her until his dying day. In short, he had hoped to marry her, had wooed her for seven long years and, as he saw it, he had been jilted by her. By his own code his 'true love' once given was hers forever. The fact that within twelve months he had bounced back, fallen in love with, and married his Charlotte was neither here nor there.

Despite their marriages, despite the complexity and bustle of his long life, despite her early death, Williamina remained his 'true love'. In this the great poet lived up to his own romantic ideal. It seemed to Scott, and he could think in no other way, that the secret sympathy that he had established with his 'true love' linked them with a silver link and a silken tie for evermore and nothing in this world, certainly not marriage, not death itself, could break that link. In love constancy was the thing. As Matilda sang:

> Perish wealth, and power and pride!
> Mortal boons by mortals given;
> But let Constancy abide,-
> Constancy's the gift of Heaven.

Scott's other heroines may have been mere shadows, but I believe they were shadows of Williamina. Unable to describe her appearance in verse during her lifetime, because he feared Williamina's ill-opinion and her censure more than anything else in the world, Scott aimed-off in his descriptions and dressed his vision of Williamina in blonde or black wigs. But the essential beauty and virtue of his heroines was always the beauty and virtue that he had first loved in Williamina. She was, as Lockhart puts it, 'the haunting dream of his manly adolescence'. Much more than that, always and everywhere, she remained Scott's ideal woman.

TO A VIOLET

The violet in her greenwood bower,
Where birchen boughs with hazels mingle,
May boast itself the fairest flower
In glen, or copse, or forest dingle

Though fair her gems of azure hue,
Beneath the dewdrop's weight reclining;
I've seen an eye of lovelier blue,
More sweet through wat'ry lustre shining.

The summer sun that dew shall dry,
Ere yet the day be past its morrow;
Nor longer in my false love's eye
Remain'd the tear of parting sorrow.

Walter Scott

*(Written in 1797, the year in which Williamina
married William Forbes.)*

The People of the Parish

Beneath those rugged elms, that yew tree's shade,
Where heaves the turf in many a mouldering heap,
Each in his narrow cell for ever laid,
The rude Forefathers of the hamlet sleep.

Thomas Gray

THE first man in Lympstone was the rector, John Prestwood Gidoin. He was parson in Lympstone from 1792 to 1820 and it is clear from the parish records that he served the parish faithfully for almost thirty years. In 1809, the year that Williamina came to be his neighbour and parishioner, he was forty-one, unmarried, and had been at the parsonage for seventeen years. Also living in the parish was his bachelor brother, James Lewis Gidoin, who was thirty-nine.

The rector presided over a complex society. His authority in the parish was absolute, but he exercised it meekly. He was loved and remembered for small kindnesses and courtesies, like the times when he would leave his carriage at home and walk with his communicants to Exeter to kneel them under the hands of the bishop and he would then treat them to plum-cake at the coffee-house in the Close before shepherding them home, rejoicing.

These two brothers had grown up together in a house at Modbury near Plymouth called Old Walls.

There they had enjoyed the moors, the river and the sea. Their father, despite his French name, was an Englishman who was seldom at home because he was busy making a fortune and rising to the rank of Admiral of the White. Their mother, Mary Legassicke, was a daughter of the local squire. She married John Lewis Gidoin at Modbury in 1763.

When Mary felt that her boys had been at home long enough, she sent them to the writing master in Plympton, and later they were packed off to the Edward VI grammar school at Tonbridge. Shortly before his eighteenth birthday, John was admitted as a pensioner at Sidney College, Cambridge where he took holy orders. Two years later his brother James entered Oriel College, Oxford.

One way and another, what with the convenient demise of bequesting Legassickes and the Admiral's accumulated prize moneys, there was wealth enough to procure the rich living at Lympstone for John, who came to the Parsonage in 1792 and lived there in great style and performed his duties, so to speak, religiously. He kept a fine carriage, saw some society and enjoyed the shooting on the commons. Four years later, after the admiral's death, his mother came to keep house for him. Neither John nor his brother James ever married but about this time James, who was by now a curate at Bigbury, became engaged to Alice Rogerson of Salcombe Regis. Alas, on 24 April 1795, they tolled the one bell only, groom there was none to see, and

Alice was buried in the place where James had thought to be married to her. This tragedy determined him to abandon his curacy and to join his family in Lympstone where he stayed until his death in 1845.

Here James ran his own household and ministered in his brother's parish. He took a leading part in parish affairs and went shooting with John and enjoyed, until death robbed him of them, the care and company of his mother and his brother. The village had two bachelor parsons, John and James, for the price of one.

His parishioners, most of them, still had their roots in the land, and agriculture was the primary source of their prosperity. The parish prized the yeomen or small farmers as patrons of some consequence able to provide shelter, warmth and sustenance in an age when there were constant shortages. Most farmers were honest, sober, and industrious, but they lived lowly and humble lives.

William Ridge at Wotton, Thomas Taylor at Combe, Peter Tillman at Pitt, such masters employed as husbandmen and as apprentices in husbandry, the poorest in the parish. Husbandmen worked through all the hours of daylight, but they fed well and slept warm. The children employed on the farms as servants often suffered a cruel servitude, but the parish knew of no better way to place bastards and orphans. The labours of peasants of all degrees kept them busy and left them little time for anything other than sleep. Most of them were unable to read or write. Even those who called themselves yeomen were often unable to sign their own names. The farmers' wives and daughters managed their households from the 'pin money' they received from poultry, pigs, and the produce of the dairy. They took pride in getting their goods to market at Exeter, whatever the weather, and in displaying their market-wares neatly.

Whatever else a man understood, he needed to know the land. The butchers and fellmongers of the parish rented fields to graze cattle, the blacksmiths needed fuel, the thatchers needed reed, the carriers, if they had orchards, would plant lucern as fodder. Even the gentry had to understand country matters - every large house had its dairy and its kitchen garden - and so too their servants. There were servants a-plenty in Lympstone, including black servants baptised late in life; such a one was James Trim. I wonder if Trim was named after the passage in *Tristram Shandy* by Thomas Sterne, when Corporal James Trim agrees that if God had left the Negro without a soul, it would be putting one sadly over the head of another. Here is the excerpt from Vol IX, Chapter six:

> 'Then do not forget, Trim,' said my uncle Toby.
> 'A negro has a soul? an' please your honour,' said the corporal (doubtingly).
> 'I am not much versed, corporal,' quoth my uncle Toby, 'in things of that kind; but I suppose, God would not leave him without one, any more than thee or me'-

'It would be putting one sadly over the head of another,' quoth the corporal.

'It would so;' said my uncle Toby.

Vol ix was first published in 1767. Parish records record that 'a black man, James Trim' was baptised in Lympstone in August 1811. Most black servants and many white had names given by their masters. I like to think whoever christened the Lympstone James Trim had this passage in mind.

Most independent of the land were the shipbuilders and shipwrights and the mariners. Fishing, like farming, was a prime source of food for the whole parish and was one of its chief industries. Mariners abounded, some in the Navy, most not. The great business of smuggling had suffered from the war with Napoleon, but there were many who recalled the trade and there were even some ancient mariners who remembered the golden age of piracy in British America. The Newfoundland trade was in decline and shipbuilding was beginning to move away from the parish, but there was a thriving coastal trade and Mr John Bass and Captain Isaac Baker, shipbuilders both, were still in business.

The lime burners were doing well in Lympstone. The coal and lime-stone to be burned arrived by ship from Torbay and the kilns were conveniently dug into the sides of Lympstone's red cliffs. Lime, the first of all artificial fertilisers, was carted away to the farms to sweeten the sandy soil of East Devon and lime-mortar was increasingly being used for building. The dangerous, reeking kilns burned day and night and needed continual tending.

The sawyer's was another important trade. The noisy sawyers rendered down the timber that the shipbuilders built into ships, the joiners into the fabric of houses, the carpenters into furniture and the coopers into barrels. Up-village, at the mill with its wide pond and its great wheel, were the busy millers and at the malt house was the maltster. Most brewing and baking was still being done at home but the innkeepers and the bakers were beginning to increase their trade. The White Swan, and the New Inn in the lower village were low, spit-and-sawdust alehouses that attracted mariners and peasants alike and offered cheap lodging to undiscriminating visitors. Out by the turnpike, Sam Darby the harness-maker had turned to innkeeping and, because the old jokes are best, he called his house The Saddler's Arms.

Saddlers and harness-makers and shoemakers and cordwainers depended on the local fellmonger for skins. The village was full of cordwainers. There were also many tailors, some of whom specialised in uniforms for the Army and the Navy. There were blacksmiths, masons, builders, gardeners, militiamen, a postmaster and a constable. Many women were lacemakers who sat at home and worked the so-called Honiton lace, and everywhere were dealers in every commodity from tobacco to toothbrushes, from green-tea to gunpowder.

Floating gracefully above this bustle there was a relatively large number of the gentry, great and small, including, Mr Pridham, the surgeon-apothecary, who understood how to inoculate against the smallpox, and a handful of Army and Naval officers, and gentlemen farmers like John Williams at Sowden whose brother, Captain Thomas Williams had been aboard *The Royal Sovereign* at Trafalgar. Then there were a few independent gentlemen like Wakelyn Welch, who was friend and adviser to the rector and the vestry. And also in the village were a handful of genteel invalids such as Lady Frances Anne Stewart Fitzroy, half-sister to Lord Castlereagh, who had recently arrived sick to death and who died here in February 1810, and, as we know, there was Williamina Forbes who had just arrived from Scotland.

At Nutwell Court, the great estate neighbouring Lympstone, lived the second Lord Heathfield. The first Lord Heathfield had been born a poor Scot within spitting distance of Branksome Hall, but had risen to become a general, a hero and a lord in that order. The second Lord Heathfield was another general but one with plenty of time to enjoy Nutwell where he bred horses and collected Dutch paintings. He was resident in the spring and summer of 1810.

In a crowded cottage in upper Lympstone lived John Nosworthy, a brother of Bill Nosworthy, the celebrated pugilist. Bill was still an apprentice baker in Exeter but he came often to Lympstone where John now acted as his manager. Young Bill already had a string of victories to his name. He had begun his career at the Haldon Racecourse as a wrestler and a boxer, then, when he was just sixteen, he had taken on and conquered the mate of a vessel at Topsham. After this began a career which took him ever farther afield. He gained famous victories at Exeter where he knocked out Perkins, a limner, and Jack Tapley, a cobbler, and in Wellington he fought and beat a local champion called Culver. In 1808, he and his brother John climbed aboard a coach to London. There his fortune had been mixed. He had fought and lost at Pancras Field, where he was carried off the ground by his brother but had fought and won at Paddington against a navigator. 'At the end of an hour the man of clay was convinced that the baker was the best man', reported Pierce Egan in *Boxiana*. Bill Nosworthy was in training for the big matches and the big purses that lay ahead. He could look forward to matches for ten guineas or even twenty-five guineas a side. All his matches were reported in the Exeter Flying Post, and the sporting fraternity in Lympstone took a personal interest in him.

At the time of Williamina's arrival in Lympstone there was a lively public battle of words being fought between John Williams of Sowden, a hot-headed gentleman-farmer, and Wakelyn Welch Esq.,

Williamina's neighbour and a gentleman who understood the law and who was the local surveyor of highways. Feelings were running high and the whole village was enjoying the row, which had lead to an exchange of letters in Trewman's *Exeter Flying Post*. The *Flying Post* was published on Thursdays at a cost of sixpence-halfpenny a copy, the same price as *The Times* of London, a sum of money that represented half of a labourer's daily wage. Copies of the *Flying Post* were passed from hand to hand around the parish throughout the week. They were read aloud to the many who could not read for themselves. No-one could ignore what the *Flying Post* said, it was the mass medium of the age.

In December 1809, J.W. wrote an impassioned letter protesting to the nobility, gentry and others of the county that Wakelyn Welsh had told him he must cut his trees back from the road connecting upper to lower Lympstone or face dire consequences. Wakelyn Welch's very cool reply appeared in the next edition. He wrote:

> SIR, A Letter published in your paper of the 14th, signed J.W. having caused an unnecessary alarm to several persons, and it having been this morning acknowledged by John Williams esq. of this place, I feel myself called upon to state my opinion, that Mr Williams has not understood any part of the question.

After a cutting analysis of the legal situation, Welch concluded:

> In performing the duties of my office, I have required Mr Williams to cut down the trees opposite to these buildings, to thin out the others, that the rest may stand about 30 feet apart; and to prune up properly those which may remain. He has had the regular requisition from me; and as soon as the time directed by the act, for waiting for his cutting them down, shall expire, I shall apply to a justice of the peace for a summons for him to attend at the next special sessions for the limit; and the parishioners of Lympston may be satisfied, that the magistrates will justly exercise that power which the act entrusts to them.
>
> I am, Sir, your most humble servant,
> W. WELCH.

It was a battle between giants but no-one in the village doubted the outcome. By the beginning of 1811 John William's trees had been felled by order of the magistrates and the timber was being offered for sale. By then, Williamina Forbes had already made the long journey back home to Scotland in her coffin.

A SOLEMN HYMN TO LYMPSTONE

Lympstone, thy skies are bright and blue,
balmy thy breezes, sweet thy showers.
Thy sun shines like a sun should do
and fills thy fields with fruits and flowers.

Like bushes grow thy salad-greens,
like big red footballs thy tomatoes,
like boomerangs thy runner-beans
and like fat pumpkins thy potatoes.

Like hedgehogs curled thy gooseb'ries grow;
brave trumpets are thy loganberries.
Like carriage-lamps thy strawb'ries glow
and brighter yet thy plums and cherries.

The fishes swimming in thy bay
are fat like pigs, fat too thy winkles
like oysters; but thine oysters, they
are huge, like dinner-plates with wrinkles.

Let other townships look for fame,
O happy Lympstone, thee we cherish
and Lympstone thou alone shalt claim
our love and duty till we perish.

Ralph Rochester

Walter and Williamina

THE KNIGHT
O lady! here, for seven long year,
Have I been nightly sighing,
Without the hope of a single tear
To pity me were I dying.

THE LADY
Should I take thee to have and to hold,
Who hast nor lands nor money?
Alas! 'tis only in flowers of gold
That married bees find honey.
Thomas Love Peacock

WALTER Scott fell in love with Williamina when she was fifteen. By this time, nineteen-year-old Walter had already managed to fall in love more than once. Indeed, he seems always to have been in love, but this time it was different; this was 'true love'. Like the poet Dante, he first glimpsed his love in church and a 'secret sympathy' for her had smitten him at a range of twenty paces. Perhaps the Dantean setting smote him in every poet's tenderest part – his longing for immortality.

Anyway, after church on one rainy Sunday in 1790, Walter dared to offer to share his umbrella with Williamina whose lovely eyes opened wide with astonishment at the audacity of his offer. She, however, blushed and accepted and he took her home, walking at her side and trying not to limp.

When she was in Edinburgh, Williamina was to be found at Greyfriars church every Sunday, and Walter, now a regular churchgoer, would walk home with her. His mother came too. Williamina wore a green cloak to church and young Walter named her 'The Lady Green Mantle'. He revealed his passion for her to his brothers and his friends. After all, what fun is there in a secret love if nobody knows about it? It transpired that her young mother knew his old mother from times past, and what was more, that their two families were distantly related. Walter Scott decided he had found the love of his life.

Walter did all that he felt a young lover should do. He concealed a medallion with her likeness around his neck, he wrote verses to her which he showed his friends and which they considered 'very poor', he went to peep at Fettercairn House where his beloved lived in summer and he carved her name in runic letters at the gate of the castle at Saint Andrews. The one thing the Lamiter could not do was to dance with the girl, but at the Assembly Rooms Williamina was happy to sit-out with him and Scott was encouraged that she should choose to sit and talk with him, hour after hour, in a corner, while all the world was capering in their view.

When Williamina was not in Edinburgh, Walter wrote letters to her at Fettercairn House and in 1795, after four years of breathless meetings, he declared his eternal love to her. The nineteen-year-old Williamina replied to this declaration like a well-conducted person. She neither committed herself nor rejected his attentions. Walter took this as more encouragement than Williamina intended and during the winter of 1795/96 the two of them met often at social occasions in Edinburgh. Nothing she said or did opened his eyes to the possibility that her love for him might not be altogether as true as his was for her.

At some stage Walter's father found out about his headstrong son's not-so-secret passion. The scrupulous father, (or was he canny?), considered the match to be hopelessly unsuitable. Williamina was an heiress and a baronet's daughter. She was more than a match for the younger son of a Writer to the Signet, and old Mr Scott smelled trouble ahead. Without telling Walter what he was about, Scott's father wrote a note of warning to Sir John (Belsches) Stuart. Sir John was not unduly bothered. He had given some time and effort to the education of Williamina and he knew his daughter to be a dutiful girl with ideas very different to those of any wild young romantic who might make verses to her eyebrows.

When in the summer of 1796 Walter was at last invited to spend a few days with Williamina's family at Fettercairn House, he arrived there hoping to impress himself upon the Stuarts as a suitable suitor. He and his friends had dreamed up a cunning plan that would result in him being at Fettercairn at the same time that his first printed book was delivered to him fresh from the printers. This book contained two translations, from the German, of ballads by Gottfried August Bürger. Walter expected, somewhat naively, that to appear at Fettercairn as a published poet would materially help his cause with Sir John and Lady Jane. The little book arrived, as he had hoped, while they were all at dinner and he was encouraged by the party to read a poem. The poem in question was his translation of *Lenore* which he called *William and Helen*. This was hardly the stuff to impress Williamina's worldly-wise father or her pious mother. It had sixty-six stanzas that concluded with Gothic ghoulishness:

> With many a shriek and cry, whiz round
> The birds of midnight scared;
> And rustling like autumnal leaves
> Unhallow'd ghosts were heard.
>
> O'er many a tomb and tombstone pale
> He spurr'd the fiery horse,
> Till sudden at an open grave
> He check'd the wondrous course.
>
> The falling gauntlet quits the rein,
> Down drops the casque of steel,
> The cuirass leaves his shrinking side,
> The spur his gory heel.

The eyes desert the naked skull,
The mould'ring flesh the bone,
Till Helen's lily arms entwine
A ghastly skeleton.

The furious barb snorts fire and foam,
And, with a fearful bound,
Dissolves at once in empty air,
And leaves her on the ground.

Half seen by fits, by fits half heard,
Pale spectres flit along,
Wheel round the maid in dismal dance
And howl the funeral song;

'E'en when the heart's with anguish cleft,
Revere the doom of Heaven!
Her soul is from her body reft;
Her spirit be forgiven.'

My guess is that even as young Walter Scott read these last dramatic words to the astounded assembly at the table, he knew that the game was up. In any case he left Fettercairn knowing only too well that he would never be received there as the accepted lover of Williamina. The days of his self-deception should have been over. I can imagine that a very critical Sir John Stuart was thinking and perhaps saying to Lady Jane, to Williamina, perhaps even to young James Mill: "The eyes desert the naked skull" indeed! Alas

for poetry! There's no great glory in that sort of thing!'
In this he would have been altogether wrong.

Six months later, Williamina married William
Forbes. The marriage pleased everybody except Scott.
Forbes was young and handsome and wealthy and
charming and Williamina knew a good man when she
saw one. She had fallen in love with him at first sight.
His shyness and his youth and his seriousness did
much for him. The two of them could bill and coo
and blush together and be serious together and her
parents approved. The idea of setting up house with
such a man and being mother to his children must have
appealed to Williamina's deep sense of duty and
propriety. All that had gone before was mere folly and
coltishness. It was time to grow up. Needless to say
Sir John and Lady Jane saw only advantages in the
connection with a great banking house and all their
neighbours nodded their heads at the essential decency
of the match. Williamina, however, knew she had some
explaining to do. She confided to William in an early
letter:

> I know that the warmth of my temper lays me open
> to errors innumerable, that I am apt to form hasty
> opinions of those whose insinuating manners or
> pleasing appearance prepossesses me in their favour.
> Altho' I have never experienced any serious
> disagreeable consequences from this fault, yet I
> have very often been much hurt and distress'd by
> finding that I had heedlessly contracted an

apparent intimacy with those whose ideas and conduct were very different from my own.

Then at some stage, perhaps in a shady, green bower, Williamina had tenderly confirmed to Scott that she would never be his. There were tears in her lovely, hazel-blue eyes because she was truly sorry for the creative romantic who had laid his heart at her feet and who was so wildly in love with her, but she did not have any doubt about what she was doing. He called her false, but she knew that she was not. She could not reproach herself. Her firm intention from now on was to love and cherish William Forbes and to be a good mother to his children. This she did, from the day that she parted from Scott until her dying day in Lympstone.

Scott soon found great gain in his great loss, which served him as an endless source of inspiration. The rise of Scott's literary star must have given Williamina and her rather reserved chosen husband, not to mention Sir John and Lady Jane, quite a lot to think about. Walter's rise must have seemed miraculous. The lame, fortuneless, rejected lover had become, decidedly and outrageously, the soul of romance and the first darling of the literate nation.

Keeping secrets wasn't in Scott's nature and just as he had managed to let his friends and family know about his love in the years when he was courting, so he contrived to let the world know about the 'true love' who was well and truly lost to him. Take this, for example, from *Peveril of the Peak,* written a dozen years after Williamina's death:

> There are few men who do not look back in secret to some period of their youth, at which a sincere and early affection was repulsed, or betrayed, or became abortive from opposing circumstances. It is these little passages of secret history, which leave a tinge of romance in every bosom, scarce permitting us, even in the most busy or the most advanced period of life, to listen with total indifference to a tale of true love.

Then too there were the letters he wrote to friends, all of whom knew of the 'Lady Green Mantle', in which he openly recalled his own great disappointment. Ultimately there were the diary entries which he surely intended for posterity. In 1825 he wrote the following dramatic entry:

> What a life mine has been! half-educated, almost wholly neglected or left to myself, stuffing my head with the most nonsensical trash, and undervalued in society for a time by my companions, getting forward and held a bold and clever fellow contrary to the opinion of all who held me a mere dreamer; broken-hearted for two years, my heart handsomely pieced again, *but the crack will remain to my dying day.*

Walter Scott

And the following year, when Sir William Forbes was helping to bail him out of debt, he wrote: 'It is fated that our planets should cross and that in periods most interesting for me. Down, down, a hundred thoughts!'

Scott was capable of sustaining more than one love and his marriage to Charlotte was not damaged by his lifelong romantic obsession with Williamina. His relationship with Charlotte seems to have been tender and affectionate. She shared his triumphs and disasters and they both rejoiced in their home and their children. But there is no doubt that he married well and truly on the rebound and that he kept his 'true love' locked away in a separate casket. The 'true love' ideal became entangled in his mind with loftier poetic ambitions and inspirations.

In 1796, in the first pangs of his disappointment, a wide range of emotions, some noble but others quite ignoble inspired Scott's fancies. Like all disappointed lovers, he dreamed of a thousand desperate acts that would restore his lost love to him, while at the same time he knew in his inner heart that nothing would avail. He spread out a veritable banquet of fancies, dreaming how he might regain Williamina; perhaps snatch her away from her unfeeling parents, prove himself a better man than her laggardly new suitor and prove the old saw that true love conquers all. For many months he stored away a treasury of romantic ideas and wild images. His fantasies were numerous enough to sustain the rest of his creative life. The rational man in him, however, knew even then that most of these ideas were 'the most nonsensical trash'.

On 17 May 1810, Williamina wrote from Lympstone to her twelve-year-old daughter Jane who had been reading stuffy and old-fashioned William Cowper while many of her contemporaries were swooning over Scott's *Lady of the Lake*.

Jane had only good things to say to her mother about the pious Cowper. (She knew of him, rather as innocent Fanny does in Jane Austen's novel *Mansfield Park*, as a sweet, simple, gentle poet and not as a suicidal lunatic with a morbid view of religion.) Williamina approved of Jane's predilection and wrote:

I am much pleased with your enjoyment of Cowper's poems. He is, as you know, a favourite author with me and I would wish you early to feel his excellence. In too many instances the language of Poetry and fiction are synonymous terms and the last property you are to expect and require of a Poet is a rigid adherence to Truth, especially when it is on his way to say *agreeable things!* For flattery is but too often considered as a necessary appendage of Poetry and rarely indeed will you meet such a poet united to such a man as Cowper presents. From this sketch you will see that *Messieurs les Poètes* are not particular favourites with me *generally speaking* but this subject and many others I now look forward to discussing with you ere long and my heart throbs at the idea.

In these few lines, Lady Forbes made terse but sufficient comment on the grand romance of Walter and Williamina. Williamina had no 'secret sympathy' for Scott. As far as she was concerned there was no 'silver link', no 'silken tie'. Romance was for her the antithesis of truth, and Williamina was not alone in her generation in believing that fiction did incalculable mischief. She was not a romantic but a practical, rational woman who had been lucky in her marriage and who owed her duty to a man she loved and respected. Scott with his sharp mind, could not have failed at any time to see all this, but in his weaker moments the poor fool played the lovelorn minstrel.

TO TIME – BY A LADY

Friend of the wretch oppressed with grief,
Whose lenient hand, though slow, supplies
The balm that lends to care relief,
That wipes her tears – that checks her sighs!

'Tis thine the wounded soul to heal
That hopeless bleeds from sorrow's smart,
From stern misfortune's shaft to steal
The barb that rankles in the heart.

What though with thee the roses fly,
And jocund youth's gay reign is o'er;
Though dimm'd the lustre of the eye,
And hope's vain dreams enchant no more?

Yet, in thy train come dove-eyed peace,
Indifference with her heart of snow;
At her cold couch, lo! sorrows cease,
No thorns beneath her roses grow.

O haste to grant thy suppliant's prayer
To me thy torpid calm impart;
Rend from my brow youth's garland fair,
But take the thorn that's in my heart.

Ah! why do fabling poets tell,
That thy fleet wings outstrip the wind?
Why feign thy course of joy the knell,
And call thy slowest pace unkind?

To me thy tedious feeble pace
Comes laden with the weight of years;
With sighs I view morn's blushing face,
And hail mild evening with my tears.

Anne Home Hunter, 1742-1821

*(These verses were among Williamina's favourites and
she is known to have recited them to Walter Scott)*

My Dearest Jane

The mind, impressible and soft, with ease
Imbibes and copies what she hears and sees,
And through life's labyrinth holds fast the clue
That Education gives her, false or true.
Plants raised with tenderness are seldom strong;
Man's coltish disposition asks the thong;
And without discipline the favourite child,
Like a neglected forester, runs wild.

William Cowper

JANE Forbes was just twelve years old when her mother
went south to Lympstone. Jane was left without father
or mother at the Forbes's home of Colinton House.
The eldest of the six Forbes children, she had a sister
and two brothers with her at home; these were Eliza,
aged nine, (with whom she shared a bed), Jack and
Charles, aged five and six. These four were under the
rule of a governess, the 'dear and good' Miss Ballingall.
The eldest of her brothers, eight-year-old William,
had already been hived off to the care of a Mr Marshall
at Peebles. Sir John Stuart and Lady Jane sometimes
drove out to see William at Peebles, and were
sometimes with their grandchildren at Colinton.
Nevertheless, Jane must often have felt very sad and
lonely.

Williamina was desperately concerned about her
children. She believed that it was her duty to her family

to exert her whole strength, under the providence of God, for their advantage and improvement and, ultimately, for the salvation of their souls; but she had little enough strength left to her. Fortunately she had an unshaken faith in the integrity and probity of Miss Ballingall. 'My dear Jane', she wrote with feeling, 'you know not, you never *can* know all that you owe to that invaluable friend! The longer you live and the more you know of others, the more you will be able to appreciate her claims on your gratitude.'

Jane was, in her mother's words, 'the farthest advanced' of the children and Williamina was determined, in so far as it was possible, to influence her daughter's education by letter, even though the post took five days to reach Colinton House. To begin with, Williamina was amused by the novelty of writing serious letters to her own child. Her first letter was boldly headed: 'LETTER To Miss Jane Forbes, Colinton House, Colinton,' and it began merrily enough: 'It gives me real pleasure, my dearest Jane, to sit down in peace and quiet to take my share in a correspondence so interesting to both of us. It is the only means in my power at present of fulfilling in any degree the personal duty I owe to you,' and goes on to give Jane some account of her journey. But subsequent letters were less jolly and began, simply, 'My dearest Jane' and they dealt first and foremost with Jane's studies and with the state of her young soul.

Williamina's education at home had been a

depressingly serious business and she intended that her own children should have an education no less rigorous and godly. This exacting attitude in no way mitigated her love for what she called her 'dear brats'. On the contrary, it was her love for them, under her love of God, that clearly dictated her duty towards them. When in the 1790s she had been studying at Fettercairn and in Edinburgh with the young James Mill for a tutor, he, who was then a devout Christian studying for the ministry, had worked her hard in the name of God and duty.

Significantly, in 1814 a few years after Williamina's death, Mill was engaged in the education of his own two eldest children. He was by then in the process of abandoning God for the sake of Utility but their education was taken no less seriously on that account. He was proud of their precocity and wrote to Francis Place:

> My two children, John and Willie, are with me at six A.M. and then we have half a day's work done before any other body is up in the house. John is now adept in the first six books of Euclid and in Algebra, performing simple questions with great ease, while in Greek he has read since he came here the last half of Thucydides, one play of Euripides and one of Sophocles, two of Aristophanes and the treatise of Plutarch on education. Willie has read along with him several lives in Cornelius Nepos, and has got over the most difficult part of the task

of learning Latin, while John wants but little of being able to read Latin with ease. His historical and other reading never stands still, he is at it whenever he has any time to spare.

At this date John Stuart Mill was, astonishingly, only just nine and his sister, seven or eight. For whatever reason, the only poet, other than the classical authors, that James ever encouraged his son to read was Walter Scott.

Jane was certainly not being ridden as hard as the young Mills and she and Eliza enjoyed their lessons and their music and their sketching, but her reading-list was nonetheless formidable. In her geographical studies she was reading the *Journey from Chester to London* by the Welsh traveller, antiquarian and natural historian, Thomas Pennant, whose works were popular towards the end of the eighteenth century. Jane had progressed as far as the salt-works and rock-salt mines of Northwich, Cheshire.

One of the first things that Williamina did after arriving in Devonshire was to visit a bookseller in Exeter, perhaps Spreats next to Spratts, and despatch a box of books to Jane. The books had arrived at Colinton by the 12 January and included a *Roman History* which Jane had long desired. But before Jane was let loose on the ancient Romans her mother wanted to impress on her that it was important for her to bear in mind that their actions must not be judged by the standard of 'revelation, for as yet the "day spring from on high" had not visited them, it must be by what is called *Natural Religion* viz. by those principles of rectitude, by that intuitive knowledge of right and wrong which God, who never left himself without a witness, has implanted in the mind of the most untutored savage if he chuses to listen to its dictates which we call conscience.' For Williamina, natural religion left much to be required, even the best Romans had no fixed principles and their virtues were pagan virtues. The mass of the people was sunk in an abyss of depravity 'while they considered themselves the only civilized people on the face of the earth and distinguished all the rest by the general name of Barbarians.'

Thus warned, Jane dived in to read about Cincinnatus, who was her favourite, and Camillus and Scipio and other Roman patricians, and about Hannibal and the Carthaginians and the Punic wars. The *Agrarian Laws* of 367BC, an early experiment in the redistribution of land, captured her imagination and she wrote to ask her landed and titled mother for an opinion. Williamina wrote in reply 'I think I once demonstrated to you the impossibility of a state of equality existing even for a short period; and altho' each man received the same share of goods at first, yet unless every member of society was endowed with the same abilities, the same bodily strength, the same health & co. & co. equality could not exist for a day.

This Miss B. will make you understand.'

Every Sunday after church, Jane, with Miss B. and Eliza, dipped into what they called their *Sunday Trembley*. Monsieur Trembley of Geneva was an eighteenth century scientist who had undertaken to give a rational Christian education to his own children and who became more and more absorbed in religion. In 1775 he published his *Instructions d'un père à ses enfans, sur la nature et sur la religion*. This, from Williamina's point of view, was a great book for children in that it taught the lesson that duty is paramount and that, by listening to his conscience, a man can know which way his duty lies. Trembley advised: 'Consult yourselves, my children; examine yourselves, notice what you think, what you feel; what you desire at present, what you hope for the future; notice what are the means that you should adopt to satisfy your desires and fulfil your hopes; notice what can lead you to your goal, what can express your feelings towards God, towards your neighbour, towards yourselves: that is religion.' Trembley also had much to say about revealed religion and about science, particularly natural history. Last but not least, because his *Instructions* were graded in difficulty as his own children grew older, they also made excellent text-books in the French language.

Down the road from their town house in Edinburgh at 53 George Street, lived Miss, she preferred Mrs, Elizabeth Hamilton, then in her fifties. Mrs Hamilton had never married, nor had she ever been a beauty, but she was a clever and godly woman and she had written several books of instruction for young people. We know that Jane was reading her books because on one occasion her mother wanted to reprimand her for 'gratifying her curiosity at the expense of her integrity'. I have no further details of this intriguing offence, but Williamina warned: 'This naturally leads me on to the leading principle of Miss Hamilton's work, the omnipresence of your great Educator and your own responsibility. The recollection of this would have spared you this error and to what are principles taught if in time of need they are to be forgotten?' There is something wonderfully cussed in this attempt of Williamina's to control the thoughts and actions of her daughter at the range of 400 miles and at intervals of at least ten days.

Jane was also reading Isaac Watts *Improvement of the Mind in Knowledge, in Religion, in the Sciences*. This was a pretty tall order for a twelve-year-old but it was a book that Williamina prized highly. She wrote: 'Read with attention and practised with care it will teach you my love the most important lesson you can learn, viz. the knowledge of your own heart, to analyze your thoughts and by tracing them to their secret springs develope at once the *motives* of your actions: that done, the principles you possess will enable you if rightly applied, to judge of your own conduct by the most unerring rules, even by the text of God's holy law.'

Although Jane was clearly already an accomplished reader, Williamina commented that her writing left much to be desired. 'My dear Jane, unless you pay very much more attention to your writing you will become a very tedious correspondent, for you require a whole side of your paper to tell me the most simple occurrence and every one circumstance must have a letter to itself; this must be the case till you are pleased to write better, as till then you cannot be allowed to attempt small hand which can alone enable you to write a letter worth reading as such.' In her next letter, Williamina told Jane to: 'Make haste and write early *small hand* that I may have *unlaborious* letters and long accounts of the Romans; for at present one of their *names* at full length would fill *a page* for you.'

When it came to inducements to conformist behaviour, Williamina had two cogent instruments which she did not hesitate to use. The first was a form of emotional blackmail. Jane, who was writing two or three letters to every one of her mother's, was told in her mother's very first letter that the next letter would depend on her conduct. 'My letters', wrote Williamina 'will be entirely ruled by the accounts Miss B. gives me; those hitherto have been entirely satisfactory and merit every reward.'

A second control was to remind Jane of the peril of her soul. Williamina would have disagreed with the gentle Sydney Smith who wrote that 'the consideration of religion may perhaps be brought too frequently before the minds of young people and a mistaken zeal may embitter the future days of a child with superstition, melancholy and terror.' When she wanted to be severe, Williamina could lay it on with a shovel. 'I should anxiously wish you my love to acquire the habit of referring all, even the most trifling of your actions, to those great principles which have with unmeasured pains have been imprinted on your mind and which (pause over the awful consideration) will assuredly be to you either the means of Grace or the sentence of condemnation!' The fires of Hell were never far away!

Even when Williamina wanted to be tender to her children, a jealous God always grabbed part of the action. This was her New Year's greeting for 1810: 'At the commencement of a New Year receive My Dearest Jane the assurance of your Mother's love, of her anxious desires her most fervent prayers for the protection of Almighty God to lead you in the way of Truth to direct you by his Grace, to support you by his Power, to redeem you by his Love, and finally my beloved children to receive you into the joy of your Lord!'

Even allowing for the spirit of the age and the fact that her thoughts were necessarily close to heaven, much of what Williamina wrote to Jane was heavy stuff. Letters were never like this in, for example, Walter Scott's family, nor yet Thomas Love Peacock's nor even in the Reverend Sydney Smith's. It is sad to think that Williamina's letters, so painstakingly composed, probably never gave Jane what she most wanted and needed; the echo of her mother's laughter, the ghost of her smile and the memory rekindled of the joy and security of her undoubted warmth. A few family jokes would have gone a long way to cheer her up, not to mention a reference to hugs and kisses. There was never much fun in Williamina's letters to Jane, although there were lots of merry quips when Williamina wrote to Sir John Stuart. There were never any drawings or sketches, despite the fact that Williamina was an accomplished artist and was sketching at Lympstone. Instead, there was a lot about God and duty, responsibility and self-sacrifice, which helps to explain just how far out Scott had been in his expectations of his 'true love'. Only for the 'Dear Babas' did Williamina send kisses.

When she grew up, Jane never married. She outlived her sister and all of her four brothers, dying in 1871 at the age of seventy-two. All her life she kept and treasured her mother's letters from Lympstone.

THE LAND'S END

At the Land's end she holds his hand;
they turn and sink the dreary land.
'Nothing of this is real,' says he
'only the rock on which we stand.'

'Above, below, it is,' says she,
'as if this space of sky and sea
is all one light, one radiant, bright
vision of how the end shall be.

'And only love is in this light,
these joyous golds, this shining white;
nothing is here that man can mend,
or make or mar, or bless or blight.'

Land's end!, world's end!, life's end!, death's end!
At last they turn again, to wend
their way up through the dreaming land,
shoulder to shoulder, hand in hand.

Ralph Rochester

The Death of Williamina

First our pleasures die and then
Our hopes, and then our fears and when
These are dead, the debt is due.
Dust claims dust – and we die too.
Percy Bysshe Shelley

As her Lympstone year progressed, Williamina felt
that a miracle was happening and that her health was
definitely improving. In February she had been too
ill even to write home and Sir William had teased her
about her looks, saying that she was 'the facsimile of a
scarecrow'. But by the beginning of March she was
feeling better than she had for the last eighteen months
and her looks were improving. Every day the carriage
was taken out and she was able to see something of
the parish and the neighbourhood. Soon she was
paying visits on foot, sometimes two in a day. She
found the weather 'beyond description charming' and
the spring flowers cheered her and she took particular
pleasure in the sweet-scented white violets. The baby,
Jem, was 'a Hercules, a sweet, merry, thriving Pet,'
and was a source of comfort and joy, and the new life
that was springing on every side disposed her heart to
cheerful thankfulness.

By the middle of May, Williamina's health seemed
to be so much improved that she and William began
to plan for the longed-for return to their home and

their loved ones at Colinton. But first they determined to make an excursion further west, to see something of Cornwall and to test whether Williamina was fit to make the long journey home. They decided to make an expedition to Land's End and then back again to Lympstone to see if she was up to the distances. It was to be a party. William's nearest and dearest brother, John Hay Forbes, had arrived to travel with them and if all went well, they would waste no time after their return before setting out again for Scotland. Williamina was confident that all would go well.

John Hay Forbes, who had been born in the same year as Williamina, was a bright young Edinburgh advocate who rose to be a judge. Later in his long life he took the title Lord Medwyn and enjoyed an estate near Peebles. He was a favourite uncle of little Jane Forbes and he came to Lympstone in the May of 1810 to give what support he could to the unwilling exiles.

Williamina's mood was so cheerful that those around her were as amazed as they were mistrusting. They recognised that remarkable phenomenon observed in consumptives, the *spes phthisica,* the hope of the consumptive, the hope of the spitter. This classic symptom of the disease was becoming ever more apparent in Williamina as every day she talked gaily of their excursion.

Jem was left in the safe care of his nurses and on the first day of June William, John and Williamina set out from Lympstone, reaching Torquay that evening.

By the end of the day, Williamina was so fatigued she could hardly take off her clothes but she put this down to the fact that the first day of a journey is always the worst. The second day she felt better and from Dartmouth they took passage on a sailing boat up to Totnes. She found sailing up the Dart, 'a sort of rest,' and found the river 'beautiful and the variety of its scenery delightful.' The only disappointment they encountered was 'sticking on a sand bank for half an hour in a most helpless state of quiescence'.

They met their carriage and reached Ivybridge at eight in the evening and the next day rumbled on to Plymouth. In a letter from Plymouth Dock to Mrs Ramage at Lympstone, Williamina added a note asking for the inventory of the house to be checked and a list to be made of all that was wanting. 'We shall have but little time at our return', she wrote.

On 8 June the Forbes were at Penzance and Williamina was in high spirits and was feeling remarkably well. She attributed her health to the influence of the journey. Nothing had done her so much good since she left Edinburgh. She found the country charming and perhaps preferable to any other part of England. From her room at their inn, she looked out and down onto the busy market-place and saw turnips bigger than both Sir William's hands, and green peas and young potatoes in a fine profusion. She was full of confidence and optimism and wrote to Jane: 'The Land's End is eight miles from this, where we mean to go today, and then return here tomorrow and propose continuing our journey towards Lympstone where we shall be, if all goes well, in two or three days. And, if it shall please God, our preparations for taking a longer journey will immediately begin which I have now the happiness of being able to look forward to with comfort as I find travelling has agreed with me so very well.'

When at last Williamina reached 'the extreme point of England's blest shores,' she was not to be discouraged from setting her foot on the last stone. 'I was not going to shrink then', she wrote the next day to Elizabeth Ramage, 'cost what it would.' It was a long way to scramble and her companions blessed themselves in silent amazement at the real fatigue she underwent. Then the little party travelled back by carriage to the inn at Marazion, Williamina congratulating herself and being nervously congratulated by the others that she had managed to do so much. They was now on the first leg of their long journey northwards, their promised journey home to Scotland. She was exhausted but she was happy and she was quite sure that a good night's rest would set all to rights.

I have not come thus far in my story without myself experiencing a certain 'secret sympathy' with Williamina Forbes. She must have been quite a girl! Everything points to the fact that she was a lady of formidable charm. Her ways were not my ways and I don't suppose the two of us would have had a lot in common, but she was certainly a plucky woman and if such remarkably different characters as Sir William Forbes and Walter Scott and James Mill could all love her, each in his own way, then I'm sure there are few men would have gone free of her enchantment.

I sincerely hope that she has managed to find her God ruling in his Episcopalian heaven in just the way that she had imagined, and that she was received into the joy of her Lord, finding the peace that she promised herself and taken her place among the saints, there to welcome Sir William and all her dear brats, even her rather spooky parents, and a host of other pious friends and relations.

I sometimes dare to remember her fondly, when I walk where she walked. The walk is still more or less here that she would have taken from the house to cross the Cliff Field, now owned by the National Trust, there to stand on the dizzy edge of the breezy cliffs and to gaze out over the muddy flats and the filling and falling tides of the wide Exe estuary. Still here too is the walk that she would have taken down the narrow path beside the Rectory garden wall to the shingle beach. Sometimes, when I go that way, her shade walks beside me and on rainy evenings I naturally offer a share in my umbrella and rejoice to see the lovely eyes open wide with astonishment at the audacity of my offer. But the image that most affects me is not here in Lympstone, it is rather the sea-girt image of her, at the Land's End. There is her carriage and there is she, with her companions, clambering down the rocky slope to the sea. Someone has talked of King Arthur, someone always does, and of Tristan and the lost land of Lyonesse. She is in good spirits and only now and then does she need a helping hand. She is short of breath and is in some pain but she will not show it. It is a fine day and there is a balmy breeze and she is with people she loves.

Now, at last, and at great cost, she is standing on the last stone of England and her anxious husband is close behind her. She stands there, with her laughing blue eyes, with the wind in her famous ringlets as though she were a figurehead set at the bows of the kingdom (a cliché of course, except that she actually did stand there.) She gazes out to sea and delights, as many do, in the vast freedom of that great ocean. Before her stretches an eternal salty space filled with light and movement and colour and with the promise of liberties and glories and adventures. Someone points the Isles of Scilly out to her, lurking like black whales on the horizon. She laughs at the triumph of it all, at the victory of having reached the ultimatum of her journey.

By the time they had limped back to Lympstone it was clear that Williamina was too ill for them ever to think of going home to Colinton. The disappointment was terrible for all the family. On the 18 June she wrote in a spidery hand her last, pathetically brave letter from

Lympstone to her son William, who was only eight years old.

My Dearest William,
Since I last wrote to you, Papa and I have made an excursion into Cornwall as far as the Lands end; which is the extreme western point of England as you will see by the Map. We had very fine weather and a very pleasant journey and I was much better for it. There are in Cornwall a number of Mines of Tin and Copper which are very curious: Mr Marshall will I am sure take the trouble of giving you some information about these if you apply to him when he is quite at leisure and do not ask silly questions. Always remember that you are much indebted to him for the attention he gives to a child like you who must often be troublesome.
I am glad that you were happy with your visit to Colinton 'tho you do not mention your brothers or your sisters in your letter. I am not a little surprized at this as you write of many things much less interesting to you and their letters do not leave you out.
I have had a little cold which is better and I hope we shall leave this place on our way home in a few days.
Papa, Mrs Ramage and James are all well and send their love,
        I am My Dearest William,
        Your affectionate Mother,
        W. Forbes.

The little household resumed its pattern of care and comfort but Williamina did not improve. As the days went by and summer drifted into autumn it was certain that she would have to stay in Devonshire over the winter, if indeed she lived that long. By the middle of September, her parents had been summoned south to Lympstone, Sir John and Lady Jane had made the long journey to be with their daughter at the last.

Some small hope lingered on. Sir John wrote for advice to Alexander Wilson, an up-and-coming medical man and a friend of the family, who was at that time, physician to the Worcester Infirmary and a fashionable practitioner in Bath. On 3 October, three days before Williamina's thirty-fourth birthday, Wilson wrote in reply, deeply regretting that he had missed them on his recent visit to Barton House at Dawlish to wait on old Admiral Schanck. Wilson disingenuously went on to say that he was happy to find, from Sir John's letter, that 'debility and not disease', was the cause of Williamina's illness, and that 'consequently the presence of Lady Jane would do much towards her certain recovery.'

The doctor's letter was small comfort. Half-hearted plans were made to travel to Bath to consult him as soon as Williamina was sufficiently recovered. Dr Wilson even sent them detailed advice as to the best route - 'the people at Taunton will endeavour to persuade you to come by Bridgewater, but do not do it!' - but by now all who tended her or sat at her bedside guessed that death was near. She lingered on and was able to make conversation until the last. Lady Jane later told James Mill how Williamina had spoken about him with almost her last breath, and had enjoined them never to allow the connection between the Stuarts and the Mills to be broken.

If Williamina spoke to her mother of Walter Scott, there is no record of it, but in 1827 Lady Jane, then a widow living in Edinburgh, wrote a singular letter to the great poet after a separation of more than thirty years, in which she asked to meet him and promised revelations: 'Age has tales to tell and sorrows to unfold'. Scott, of course, could not refuse and he met her several times. After the first of these occasions he wrote in his journal: 'I went to make a visit, and fairly softened myself like an old fool, with recalling old stories, till I was fit for nothing but shedding tears and repeating verses for the whole night. This is sad work. The very grave gives up its dead, and time rolls back thirty years to add to my perplexities.' There can be little doubt that Lady Jane told him and re-told him of the death-bed scene in Lympstone. It was on this occasion too that he copied out the lines *To Time – by a Lady,* a poem that had been a favourite with Williamina.

Alas! once again, regrettably but inevitably, both James Mill and Walter Scott had managed to intrude on the private world of Sir William Forbes. It was William who watched over her for a year, anxious at

Sir William Forbes

her uneven breathing, alarmed by her sporadic coughing, who sat long hours at her bedside, who held her hand, and who gave her what comfort he could. To his unspeakable grief, Williamina died in the early hours of 5 December.

It was a biting cold night. At four o'clock in the morning the young sexton John Venman was winkled out of bed to muffle the clapper of the great bell and to toll the knell for the death of Lady Forbes.

THE DEATH-BED

We watch'd her breathing through the night,
Her breathing soft and low,
As in her breast the wave of life
Kept heaving to and fro.

So silently we seem'd to speak,
So slowly moved about,
As we had lent her half our powers
To eke her living out.

Our very hopes belied our fears,
Our fears our hopes belied —
We thought her dying when she slept,
and sleeping when she died.

For when the morn came dim and sad,
And chill with early showers,
Her quiet eyelids closed — she had
Another morn than ours.

Thomas Hood

Lympstone and Beyond

All help is vain! My final hour draws near!
Parent belov'd, my King, my Father dear!
But when these eyes no more Amelia see,
Though the cold grave enclose, Remember me!
From The Gentlemen's Magazine, 1812

GEORGE III's youngest daughter, the Princess Amelia, died a month before Williamina did. The Princess was her father's favourite and her last words to him were 'remember me, father, but do not grieve for me'. The Princess's illness and death brought the king first to despair and then to madness, again. His mind ghosted away and from 5 February 1811, the kingdom was ruled by his regent, George, Prince of Wales.

At Lympstone, one of the first transactions of the Regency was the sale by auction advertised by Mr Abraham Stogdon, churchwarden on February 16 of the fine house lately in the possession of Sir William Forbes Bart. The auction took place in the lower village at the New Inn on 11 March and the fee-simple and inheritance of the house passed to a local family, that of the Captain of the Port of Gibraltar, William Sweetland.

Williamina's brief tenure was like a barely-perceptible short, scarlet thread in the great tapestry that was Lympstone society. She was no sooner gone than she was forgotten. The ten years that followed her death saw no dramatic changes in the parish and yet society was changing fundamentally. The tides ebbed and flowed and the seamen and fishermen at one end of the parish and the peasants at the other remained as miserably poor and diseased as before. But slowly, slowly, a common consciousness was emerging that all men could and should live better, more gentle, lives. The March of Mind was marching into Lympstone and bringing ideas about the dissemination of knowledge and of the possibility of universal literacy. The work of the great reformers like James Mill had much to do with these changes, but so too did the availability of popular literature. (The rector baptised his first Walter in 1819). When peace came in 1815 it cooled the ardour of patriots and allowed long suppressed doubts to be expressed. The old rector's authority was increasingly questioned by the various dissenters who had once lived in such fear of repression that their meeting-houses, such as the one at Gulliford, were built in remote corners at the parish boundaries. In general, there was a new confidence abroad among the common people. The great lords no longer appeared quite so great, nor did the gentry appear so unapproachably genteel.

Of those who had cared for Williamina, all except Georgiana Reynolds returned to Scotland. Georgiana lived in Lympstone to a ripe old age and had many babies, most of whom died in infancy. Elizabeth Ramage became housekeeper at Drumlanrig Castle, home to the Dukes of Buccleuch. She was there when Walter Scott visited in 1826. Later she married a Mr Black, who made her a widow for the second time. Sir William Forbes returned to Colinton heart-broken by Williamina's death. Sir John and Lady Jane both died in Scotland. As for what happened to the baby, Jem, well, he shall have an opportunity to speak for himself.

The rector of Lympstone, The Reverend John Prestwood Gidoin, became domestic chaplain to William Legge, the new, young Earl of Dartmouth, who was famous at Eton for his handsome looks and was eulogised by a schoolfellow as: 'Mild as the dew that whitens yonder plain / Legge shines serenest 'midst your youthful train.' The mild and serene-shining earl seems to have made few if any demands on his domestic chaplain but the patronage of that noble lord was welcomed by the parish as a pretty compliment and a confirmation of its essential gentility.

Neither the war with America nor the assassination of the First Minister, Mr Perceval, nor the little local earthquake that shook the houses and sent villagers scurrying from their beds at six in the morning on Sunday 21 March 1813 made much impression on the parishioners of Lympstone. Nor did they pay much heed to the tremors when the news travelled down from London that the second Lord Heathfield, the aged owner of Nutwell Court, had died earlier that year. Yet, as a direct consequence of this death a row was brewing which would keep the parish chattering and the vestry busy for a while. This was the Battle of the Pews.

For most of the eighteenth century, Nutwell had been the home of Sir Francis Henry Drake, a direct descendant, give or take a few inches, of the great Devon hero. When Sir Francis Henry died the Nutwell estate passed to his nephew, the second Lord Heathfield, a zealous general, who inherited his glorious title as Lord Heathfield, Baron of Gibraltar from his father.

This father had been General Eliott, the Hero of the Siege of Gibraltar and, as his memorial tells us: 'The spectacle which he... there exhibited to the eyes of France and Spain and to an Amphitheatre of Princes who beheld the glorious Scene will be an Eternal Memorial of British Courage and British Humanity.'

The second Lord Heathfield was proud of his father's achievements and counted them with his own and he wonderfully ornamented the Lympstone lodge to his Nutwell estate with a chimney pot fantastically designed in the form of the castle and key, the symbols of Gibraltar and the device of the Barons of Gibraltar.

Lord Heathfield's heir was a young captain of light infantry called Thomas Trayton Fuller. It was he who was to be frustrated in Lympstone's Battle of the Pews. Thomas Fuller, now calling himself Captain Drake, turned up to enjoy his new estates in Devonshire in the summer of 1813. His regiment was still in the Peninsula preparing to cross the Pyrenees but Captain Drake had said goodbye to all that. To the horror and dismay of the whole parish, he promptly gave orders that 'locks should be put upon the Doors of certain Pews in Lympston Church, and, the following Sunday, he occupied by his Family, Servants and Tenants four pews in Lympston Church preventing several Parishioners of Lympston who had been used to sit in certain of those Pews from being accommodated with sittings therein.'

This high-handed invasion of the church was a serious matter. These pews had been assigned to householders of the parish by the vestry and nothing less than the authority of the rector was at stake. The incomer, Captain Drake, was hoping to reclaim ancient rights that pre-dated a system which had for many years produced necessary funds for parish relief. The case was complex and the parish needed a good man to guide them through the legal maze. Wakelyn Welch Esq. rose to the occasion. He corresponded with Captain Drake's steward and wrote to Doctors Commons to seek the erudite opinion of counsel and had a very busy, happy time of it. At length a compromise was reached that satisfied both parties and in February 1814 the relevant documents were placed in the parish chest and the vestry thanked Wakelyn Welch for the 'unwearied exertions and the steady perseverance by which he had asserted the rights of the parish'. The outcome of the Battle of the Pews, although it was not a decisive victory for the parish, showed the world that the vestry was not composed entirely of clodhoppers and the parish had done enough to discourage Captain Drake of Nutwell Court, or any of his successors, from ever again interfering in Lympstone's affairs.

Bill Nosworthy also fought a famous battle in 1814. He had reached the heights of his profession and his opponent was the celebrated Jewish fighter, Dutch Sam, champion of champions, who was expected to dispose of the young clod-poll from Devon in no time. Dutch Sam had an awesome reputation. It was said that to be hit by him was 'like unto a thousand bugs crawling up and down the ear of a man'. Sam and Bill met before a record crowd at Mousley Hurst on Tuesday 8 December. Nosworthy emerged victorious after a long, slogging match. The result was so unexpected that 'the abdication of Bonaparte, in its proper sphere, was not more electric than the defeat of Dutch Sam, in the boxing world', according to Pierce Egan. There were some glorious fights and riots among those who had bet on the result.

Before the fight Dutch Sam was reported as saying to Nosworthy: 'So help my Cot! Bill, I will not only fight you first and beat you, but I will afterwards take you home, and nurse you like one of my own children!'

To this Nosworthy replied that he thanked Sam for his kindness but that Sam had not beat him yet and that there was not a Jew amongst them who could accomplish that task. After the fight Bill visited the damaged Sam who was bolstered up in bed. 'Sam', said he, 'did I beat you or did I not?' Sam sorrowfully answered: 'By Cot! Bill, you did, against my will! I would have knocked your head off if I could, but in that small ring you never gave me a chance to win.'

It was a famous victory and it was widely reported and earned Bill his place in Pierce Egan's *Boxiana*. It brought him great acclaim and small fortune and further fights in which he suffered terrible injuries. In the autumn of 1816 he was brought back to Lympstone a broken man to die at his brother John's house on 26 October. He was only thirty years old. A month later, a shining new Bill Nosworthy, infant son of John and Mary, was baptised by the rector of Lympstone.

In 1815, at the even more famous victory at Waterloo, Lympstone was represented by young John Haddy James, whose mother was a sister of John Williams of Sowden - John Williams of the trees. James enlisted as a surgeon, witnessed the battle and was then with the army in Paris. He came back safe and sound to Lympstone to woo Elizabeth Withall and to take her to wife. James went on to become a famous doctor at Exeter where his portrait still hangs in the hospital. A hundred years after his death, his Waterloo journal in which he gave a graphic account of the campaign, was discovered tucked away under the eaves of a Lympstone apple-loft. It was published to the world.

There are now some very small parochial matters to attend to, but the world should surely not be allowed to forget how in September 1816, 'the lady of R. Welland Esq. R.N. of Lympston' was delivered of twin daughters. This confinement was her fourteenth. Or how in September 1819, William Jackson, blacksmith, and Ann his wife, christened their latest son, William Wellington Waterloo Jackson.

On St George's Day, 1818, Wakelyn Welch died and gave to the parish £200 for the purchase of blankets each Christmas as loans to poor cottagers, plus £100 for the instruction of poor children, in Sunday School or otherwise. Five years later, his widow Elizabeth died and left funds to the parish to build a school near the church in his memory. Lympstone Primary School still occupies the site.

In the winter of 1819 the Duke of Kent came to Sidmouth. With him were the Duchess and the infant Princess Victoria, she who would one day be Queen and Empress. Here a careless boy nearly deprived Britain of the Victorian age. He had gone out to shoot small birds and somehow he mistook the royal baby for a cock-sparrow. The glass of the nursery window was shattered and some of the shot passed close to the head of the child in the nurse's arms. The Duke and Duchess were not amused, but they let the boy go home when he promised never again to shoot at royal babies. A few days later the Duke of Kent died. He would no doubt have lived if he had taken the advice of Captain Conroy with whom he had been out for a long walk. Conroy suggested to the Duke that he ought not to delay changing out of his wet boots, but the Duke lingered a while to bounce his chubby infant daughter on his knee. This was fatal. The Duke died on Sunday the 23 January 1820 and was embalmed by Mr Luscombe, a surgeon of Exeter, who made so good a job of the Duke that he was later offered the choice of a knighthood or two thousand guineas by Queen Victoria. He took the guineas. That same week, John Prestwood Gidoin died.

The same newspapers that recorded the Duke of Kent's death offered these notices to the people of Devon:

> On Tuesday, at the Parsonage House, Lympstone, died of apoplexy, the Rev. John Prestwood Gidoin, rector of that place; to the unspeakable grief and regret of all who were blessed with his friendship, and particularly those who had been trained by his precepts and example in the paths of virtue and religion. While genuine and unaffected worth and true piety continue to be honoured among men the memory of this excellent man will be cherished in the hearts of all who knew him. This is inserted by desire of one who in her early years had the happiness of being one of his flock.

The remains of the late J.P. Gidoin, Rector of Lympstone, were interred in the family vault in the parish church. The very numerous attendance of his parishioners and friends on the melancholy occasion evinced their high regard and respect. His nearest relative will have to deplore the loss of an only and affectionate brother and the poor a warm and zealous friend.

The Regency was a grand age for hyperbolic epitaphs, but there is a ring of sincerity in these for Lympstone's rector that I find deeply moving. In any case, it was an end of an era. Three days later at Windsor, mad King George III died. His last words were: 'Poor Tom's a-cold!'

I was that Baby!

It is a modest creed, and yet
Pleasant if one considers it,
To own that death itself must be,
Like all the rest, a mockery.

That garden sweet, that lady fair,
And all sweet shapes and odours there,
In truth have never passed away:
'Tis we, 'tis ours, are changed; not they.
Percy Bysshe Shelley

WILLIAMINA'S mortal remains were conveyed at once to Scotland and baby Jem was soon reunited with his brothers and sisters at Colinton. There, the bereaved family closed its gates against the cruel world and mourned the death of Williamina. Sir William was inconsolable. He lived for another sixteen years but, according to all accounts, he never recovered from his great loss.

Jem was a bright, precocious baby. His sister Jane remembered him dancing wildly at the nursery window, altogether fascinated by the spectacle of Halley's comet which appeared in 1811 when he was two years old. She quoted this as an early evidence of his remarkable interest in scientific subjects. More convincing evidence was her memory of him at an age when most children are still glued to their teddybears lugging a red-backed almanac everywhere he went which his brothers and sisters called Jem's Red Brother. In this book, the boy kept faithful records of barometer and thermometer readings - as indeed his mother had done in Lympstone.

Despite his early bloom, Jem proved to be a sickly child and it was soon accepted that he was Sir William's particular favourite, not only because he was the youngest and most delicate of the children, but because he was his father's last link with Williamina. Sir William decreed that Jem was not to be sent to school and that Charles should also be educated at home, primarily so that Jem might have some company. Young William and Jack, on the other hand, were sent away to be educated in England.

The two younger boys were taught by the same beloved Miss Ballingall who had taught Jane and Eliza and by their father, who taught them Latin. Every schoolday evening from when Jem was nine, he and Charles rode from the house to the village of Colinton where they were given after-school lessons by the parish schoolmaster. Jane and Eliza and Charles were effectively the only companions of his childhood and his affection for them was accordingly intense and lifelong.

But the person that Jem cared for most in the world was his broken-spirited father. When Jem was fifteen Sir William made clear that he wished his son to qualify for the Scottish bar. Both Sir William and Jem's uncle, John Hay Forbes, now already a judge, had qualified as barristers at Edinburgh University and the law was deemed the safest and most lucrative profession that any young man could aspire to. Jem, however, was no lover of the law. He had already set his heart on becoming either a clergyman or a scientist; but because he was, in Jane's words, a gentle and docile boy, he did not quarrel with his father. From the age of sixteen, with diligence but without enthusiasm, he studied law at Edinburgh. Remarkably, by the time he was twenty-two, he had not only completed his legal studies, but had at the same time established himself as a scientist by writing erudite articles for the *Edinburgh Journal of Science* under a pseudonym.

In the summer of the year 1826 when Jem was eighteen, Sir William took all his children to the Continent on a form of Grand Tour. This was a remarkable undertaking and one that should have served as a monument to his love and the family's essential solidarity and happiness, but tragedy struck at Malta, where young William, the son and heir, fell ill and died at the age of twenty-four. The Forbes continued their tour but Sir William, who was even then not reconciled to the loss of Williamina, was visibly shattered by this second loss. He never recovered from it and died two years later at the age of fifty-seven.

Jem, (though now I must call him James), tried to make some assessment of his father's life after

Lympstone. At the age of thirty he wrote: 'My father was almost distracted by his loss: a man of the most virtuous, amiable, high-minded, and singularly unobtrusive disposition, he was evidently formed for the complete enjoyment of domestic happiness. He had, it appears, so concentrated his affections on my mother, that with her loss he was a changed man: he lived as a Christian ought to do, striving to fulfil his duty to his family and to mankind by the most active but generally secret benevolence; but from the time of my mother's death I suppose no one shared his entire confidence.'

Here, *à propos* 'secret benevolence', let it be noted that it was only after Sir William's death that Walter Scott, then Sir Walter, learned for the first time that his old friend and rival had absorbed a credit demand for over £2,000, thus removing some significant part of the famous burden of debt that Scott was carrying.

James was twenty when his father died. His brother Jack now became the eighth baronet of Pitsligo, and James, who had scarcely been separated from his father all his life, struggled on to complete his legal training out of a sense of duty to the parent he loved and admired. No sooner, however, had he qualified than he shelved his law books and gave all his attention to his scientific studies. His special interest was in glaciers and he went on to become an accomplished mountaineer. So brilliant were his studies that the next year he was elected, at the remarkably young age of twenty-four, to the Chair of Natural Philosophy at the University of Edinburgh and many years later he became Principal of the United College of the University of St. Andrews.

The year after he had been elected professor, James' summer tour took him to the Isle of Wight and then to the South West of England. He was resolved that he would visit Lympstone again and so, on midsummer's day 1834, he came walking from Exmouth along the banks of the Exe, back into the village that he had left in 1810. He was a tall, dark-haired, young man, thin almost to the point of emaciation and with a narrow, serious face. His visit was a pilgrimage but, as always, he made his scientist's neat, precise notes in his journal. At Lympstone he wandered about where the father he loved and the mother he never knew had walked before him. He noted that John Prestwood Gidoin and Wakelyn Welch had died, and he made a neat thumbnail sketch of The House. He thought fondly of his long dead mother and of his father and of their year in this place. The quotation *et haec olim meminisse iuvabit*, 'the day may dawn when this shall be sweet to remember', from Virgil's *Aeneid* came to mind and he jotted it down in his journal.

The next morning he wrote to his sister Jane from the Old London Inn at Exeter and included a neat sketch-map showing the precise location of the house where Williamina had died and of which he had been 'the almost unconscious inhabitant' twenty-four years before.

Dear Jane

I wrote to Eliza from Exmouth and told her how much I was pleased with Devonshire and its scenery. It has much more than equalled my expectations and though the weather has not been particularly settled, not being in a hurry, I get on very well. How anyone can see this country without either walking or riding I do not understand. At least excursions must be made from the various points. Yet a pedestrian is rather a curiosity here and seeing that people gradually stared I have enquired whether such animals are scarce and am informed that they are.

Accordingly at Lympstone, which I entered yesterday on a fine morning, the people looked very much astonished to see a person, who looked as if he could afford to pay for at least an outside place, walk into a town through which 2 coaches pass daily. You may conceive better than I can describe my feelings at that moment. For some days my sympathies had gradually been warming towards a point in which I felt so deep and melancholy an interest. It is but rarely that in the life of a sober man this species of Interest can be so fairly worked up as in my case. I left Exmouth early in the morning and sauntered up the bank of the Exe under a melancholy sky and with somewhat excited feelings determined not easily to forgo the object of finding the spot where my parents lived tho' by no means sure how I should easily effect it.

I walked almost through the village without seeing anything like a communicative face – I almost fancied I should have been received as a known face – instead of being an object of not a little curiosity – at length I enquired for the church which is not very conspicuous and, as I expected, found an old Sexton who I thought might be a chronicler of more than 24 years back. – I soon entered into conversation with him – found that he recollected the individuals in question, nay, the first thing he told me was that he had with his own hands tolled the bell at 4 in the morning on our poor mother's death. Like most of his trade he was not of very fine feelings – but he was communicative and you may imagine the impression which his little anecdotes as fresh as of yesterday made upon me. I made him take me to the top of the church tower and shew me the house where they lived and those of the neighbours about the fate of some of whom I enquired... I made him shew me where they sat in church and I walked from the church to the house by the very path leading also to the parsonage which they had often trod. It seemed a sort of hallowed ground. The house is now occupied by a Mr. Sweetland and is in excellent repair. It has nothing very prepossessing in the exterior – except in plain neatness. I wished I could have had our mother's letters to collate them on the spot. You may recollect the interest I took in them when you were so good as to send them to me. I copied them with such a species of veneration that I retained not merely word for word but page for page and line for line. Of course I felt a peculiar and additional interest in everything on the spot from considering that I was not visiting these places for the first time – that I had been the almost unconscious inhabitant of this very house. Nor could I help speculating upon what identity subsisted between my then and my present state of existence. The old Sexton recollected the Baby and certainly was somewhat moved when I said 'I am that Baby.' – I strolled from the church to the House and from the house to the church and could hardly tear myself away which I did too late to avoid an impending thunderstorm.

James had slipped up. Or had he? Georgiana Reynolds who had cared for him and for his mother and had bounced him on her knee was still living here in 1834 and so was James Lewis Gidoin, the rector's brother, both of whom would have remembered Sir William and Lady Forbes and would have rejoiced to see what had become of baby Jem. But James, for all his success and scholarship, was just as much a mimosa as was his father before him and he wanted only to be alone with his thoughts. I suspect he could not have borne to hear more of the story than he already knew. It was enough for him to pace up and down, wild-

James David Forbes aged two

eyed and close to tears, from house to church, from church to house again, knowing that it was here that the mother he loved but could not remember, had once hung on his father's arm.

James David Forbes went on to become the foremost British expert on glaciology. In 1843 he was the author of *Travels through the Alps of Savoy and other parts of the Pennine Chain with observations on the phenomena of Glaciers through the Alps*, and, in 1859 of the ground-breaking - what else? - *Occasional Papers on the Theory of Glaciers*. In 1843 he married. There can be no doubt that his mother would have been proud of him.

So much for Baby Jem. It is more difficult for me to part from my heroine, Williamina. Her spirit clings. Who knows? Perhaps those poets are right who believe that love, beauty and delight somehow defy death and change. Perhaps her presence in Lympstone shall never altogether pass away.

Williamina was loved by three remarkable men. She was adored by Walter Scott and she had been hardly less desired by James Mill. Sir William Forbes, who was more sensitive by far than the great poet and more human by far than the great reformer, won her and merited her and was happy in her love. After she died, while Scott's aching heart was still bringing him fame and fortune, while James Mill was busy reforming mankind and bullying his wife and children, William Forbes could not find the words to speak to anybody about his lost love. He had loved Williamina truly and he mourned her truly until the day he died.

'And now, 'tis silent all!
– Enchantress, fare thee well!'

FAREWELL TO THE MUSE

Enchantress, farewell, who so oft hast decoy'd me,
At the close of the evening through woodlands to
roam,
Where the forester, 'lated, with wonder espied me
Explore the wild scenes he was quitting for home.
Farewell and take with thee thy numbers wild
speaking
The language alternate of rapture and woe:
Oh! none but some lover, whose heartstrings are
breaking,
The pang that I feel at our parting can know.

Each joy thou couldst double, and when there came
sorrow,
Or pale disappointment to darken my way,
What voice was like thine, that could sing of
to-morrow,
Till forgot in the strain was the grief of to-day!
But when friends drop around us in life's weary
waning,
The grief, Queen of Numbers, thou canst not
assuage;
Nor the gradual estrangement of those yet
remaining,
The languor of pain, and the chillness of age.

'Twas thou that once taught me, in accents
                            bewailing,
To sing how a warrior lay stretch'd on the plain,
And a maiden hung oe'r him with aid unavailing,
  And held to his lips the cold goblet in vain;
As vain thy enchantments, O Queen of wild
                            Numbers,
  To a bard when the reign of his fancy is o'er,
And the quick pulse of feeling in apathy slumbers —
Farewell, then, Enchantress! I meet thee no more.

Sir Walter Scott

*(Written in 1822. The warrior of the third stanza is
Marmion, the maiden is the Lady Clare.)*

FURTHER READING:

There is unpublished material at both the University of St Andrew's and the National Library of Scotland. There are Forbes Papers and Fettercairn Papers. Both include some of Williamina's letters from Lympstone.

James Mill, a Biography by Alexander Bain (Longmans, 1882). The standard biography.

James David Forbes, Pioneer Scottish Glaciologist by Frank F. Cunningham, (Scottish Academic Press, 1990).

Life of Sir Walter Scott by Sir Walter's son-in-law, John Gibson Lockhart (Charles and Adam Black, 1878) is still the best biography of the great man.

The Wizard of the North, The Life of Walter Scott by Carola Oman (Hodder & Stoughton, 1973). Has a good chapter about Greenmantle (sic) aka. Williamina.

The Poetical Works of Sir Walter Scott with the Author's Introductions and Notes edited by J. Logie Robertson (Oxford University Press, 1926). Lots of romantic poems, long and short, all of which are out of fashion, but why be a sheep?

Redgauntlet, A Tale of the Eighteenth Century by Sir Walter Scott (Constable, 1824 and many editions since). Green Mantle, the novel's heroine, is based on young Williamina.

James David Forbes, FRS by John Campbell Shairp, Peter Guthrie Tait and A. Adams-Reilly (Macmillan, 1873). Features a charming portrait of Forbes aged two.

BOOKS ABOUT DEVON:

Woodbury, A View from the Beacon by Ursula W. Brighouse (A Woodbury News Publication, 1981) is a classic parish history and a joy to read.

The Raleigh Country by Eric R. Delderfield (ERD Publications 1949, revised 1966).

Devon by Professor W.G. Hoskins (David and Charles, 1978) is a revised edition of the foremost historical study of the county.

Lympstone, A Village Story by Elizabeth Scott (Transactions of the Devonshire Association Vol. 88, 1956).

From Trackway to Turnpike by Gilbert Sheldon (Sheldon, 1928). Gives a good account of the history of East Devon's lanes and highways. Sheldon was a poet, novelist and historian, and a friend of Walter de la Mare. He lived and wrote at Williamina's house in Lympstone in the early years of the twentieth century.

A Devon Anthology chosen by Jack Simmons (Macmillan, 1971). A pleasing collection of literary bits. *The Lympstone Story, The Red Cliffs of Lympstone* edited

by Rosemary Smith (The Lympstone Society, 1995).
Picturesque Sketches of the Churches of Devon by William
Spreat (Spreat, 1842).

The Rise of the Devon Sea-Side Resorts, 1750-1900 by
John E. Travis (University of Exeter Press, 1993).
Detailed study of Devon resorts, including their role in
providing accommodation for invalids.

A General View of the Agriculture of the County of Devon
by Charles Vancouver (1808). This fascinating book was
reprinted in facsimile by David and Charles in 1969.

Lympstone Parish Records and Vestry Minutes can be
examined at the West Country Studies Library in Castle
Street, Exeter.

OTHER BOOKS OF INTEREST:

Boxiana, or Sketches of Antient and Modern Pugilism by
Pierce Egan (John Bell, 1818–1821) gives a blow-by-blow
account of Bill Nosworthy's career as well as a lively
account of other Regency boxers.

Surgeon James' Journal 1815, by John Haddy James,
edited by Jane Vansittart (Cassell, 1964).

Redcliff by Eden Phillpotts (Hutchinson, 1924). A novel
which gives a lively picture of Lympstone and
Lympstone society in the 1920s.

ABOUT AGRE:

Agre Books is a small, independent publisher which specialises in non-fiction books of literary merit about South West subjects. Based in Dorset, it covers the South West peninsula.

Agre takes its name from the legend of Actaeon and Diana as told in Ovid's *Metamorphoses*. Ovid names Actaeon's hounds and lists their attributes. 'The thicket searcher Agre' was the hound with the keenest nose. Agre Books intends to search the thickets of its distinctly rural region to find interesting truths and intriguing stories.

Titles published include:

Bridgwater – The Parrett's Mouth (£9.99). Poems and notes by James Crowden, plus fifty black and white photographs by Pauline Rook taken to mark the 800th anniversary of the town's charter. This unusual book captures the essence of a community and its surrounding countryside.

Islomania (£6.50) by Sara Hudston with photographs from the Gibson Archive on the Isles of Scilly. Islomania - an obsession with islands. Why are islands so captivating? Using Scilly as its example, this book explores what islands mean to us.

The Wheal of Hope (£9.99). Poems and notes by James Crowden, photographs by George Wright. The closure of South Crofty tin mine marked the end of 3,000 years of Cornish history. Wright and Crowden record the mine's last months.

FORTHCOMING FROM AGRE:
The Cornish Pasty by Stephen Hall. An illustrated and entertaining account of the original fast food. Includes authentic recipes never before published alongside details of pasty making past and present, the pasty overseas and pasty myths and legends.

The Little Commonwealth by Judith Stinton. In the 1910s psychologist Homer Lane opened a remarkable experimental school in a remote Dorset hamlet. Using new material never before published, this account reveals the truth about the community that influenced educational pioneer A.S. Neill.

To find out more about Agre you can write to Agre Books, Groom's Cottage, Nettlecombe, Bridport, Dorset, DT6 3SS. You can read extracts from books and discover more about Agre's authors by visiting the website at www.agrebooks.co.uk.

ABOUT THE PRINTING OF THIS BOOK:
For Love of Williamina was typeset by Agre Books in Monotype Imprint, plus Snell Roundhand and Trajan. The cover was designed by Stuart Brill at Senate Design Ltd in London. The book was printed and bound on 80gsm Clan Bookwove Antique White Vol 17.5 by R. Booth (Bookbinders) Ltd of Mabe, near Penryn in Cornwall. Booth's was founded as a bookbinder's by Robert and Mary Booth in 1971. In 1977 their son Steven joined the business and the firm expanded into printing.

ABOUT THE AUTHOR:

Ralph Rochester was born in Liverpool in 1939 and now lives in Lympstone. In 1995 he won first prize in *The Independent*/Scholastic Story of the Year Competition. He served for many years in the army, his last tour of duty being in Bosnia for the UN. Major Rochester is also the sole begetter of Henry Hogge's *Pig Poets, - Porcine Parody for Pig-Lovers* (HarperCollins, 1995). His poetry has appeared in many anthologies and journals, including *The Literary Review*. He keeps a small boat on the River Exe and, when the tide is right, enjoys rowing to a nearby pub.